Actual Experiences of a CEO

Actual Experiences of a CEO

How to Make Continuous Improvement in Manufacturing Succeed for Your Company

Hank McHale

ASQC Quality Press
Milwaukee, Wisconsin

Actual Experiences of a CEO: How to Make Continuous Improvement Succeed for Your Company
Hank McHale

Library of Congress Cataloging-in-Publication Data

McHale, Hank, 1938–
    Actual experiences of a CEO: how to make continuous improvement
in manufacturing succeed for your company / Hank McHale.
        p.   cm.
    Includes bibliographical references and index.
    ISBN 0-87389-329-8 (alk. paper)
    1. Production management.   2. Quality control.   3. Total quality
management.   I. Title.
TS155.M3457   1995
658.5—dc20   95-2536
                                                         CIP

10 9 8 7 6 5 4 3 2 1

ISBN 0-87389-329-8

Acquisitions Editor: Susan Westergard
Project Editor: Kelley Cardinal

ASQC Mission: To facilitate continuous improvement and increase customer satisfaction by identifying, communicating, and promoting the use of quality principles, concepts, and technologies; and thereby be recognized throughout the world as the leading authority on, and champion for, quality.

For a free copy of the ASQC Quality Press Publications Catalog, including ASQC membership information, call 800-248-1946.

Printed in the United States of America

  Printed on acid-free recycled paper

ASQC
Quality Press
611 East Wisconsin Avenue
Milwaukee, Wisconsin 53202

Contents

Foreword

Hank McHale brings to us in *Actual Experiences of a CEO: How to Make Continuous Improvement in Manufacturing Succeed for Your Company* a welcome discourse on essentials to the success of manufacturing improvement. I have never had the opportunity to read about continuous improvement in manufacturing from other than the perspective of a technocrat. This book discusses the subject from the important perspective of a fellow chief executive officer.

Technically rigorous and thoughtfully done, the book serves as a teaching aid, an on-the-job reference guide, and a source of general information. I especially found the chapters on root-cause analysis to be highly relevant. All too often, time is not taken to get to the root cause of issues, only resulting in a recurrence of the problems.

The chapters flow well and can be read either in sequence or as individual case studies relating to continuous improvement in manufacturing. While the book is written from an experience base of basic manufacturing, primarily metal forming and associated products, I believe that it will be found to be broadly relevant across all manufacturing environments as well as the service industries.

There are numerous, well-documented practical examples, including informative discussions of what works and doesn't work, so the reader has a chance to learn by someone else's experiences. The book also has a uniquely thoughtful perspective on customer needs and supplier costs, with excellent examples of win–win efforts—essential for success in today's partnerships.

I found the book to be quite balanced. It is technical enough to contain more than broad generalizations, yet broad enough that the reader does not miss the main themes because of unnecessary technical detail.

At Northwestern Steel and Wire Company, where continuous improvement is our constant goal, we are looking forward to sharing Hank McHale's perspectives, just as we have recently shared the ideas expressed in Tom Peters' *Liberation Management* and Michael Hammer and James Champy's *Reengineering the Corporation*.

Robert N. Gurnitz
Chairman, President, and Chief Executive Officer
Northwestern Steel and Wire Company
Rockford, Illinois

Acknowledgments

Many people have influenced this book. Many friends and business associates spent valuable time offering suggestions and ideas that have substantially improved various drafts. I am particularly grateful to Mike Beckman and Jeff Jackson, both executives at GO/DAN Industries who possess valuable experience and knowledge of manufacturing, for their honesty and for continually pressing me for clarity and to share more of my experiences. My appreciation also goes to ASQC reviewers whose insightful critiques forced many of my thoughts into sharper focus.

My thanks also go to various executives at Rockwell International's Automotive Operations for taking the unprecedented step of allowing a marketing staff executive to start a manufacturing career by appointing me materials manager of two axle plants, even though they must have expected I was going to make mistakes, which I did.

I am also grateful to my wife, Mimi, who offered support and encouragement, particularly since much of this book was written on vacations and weekends. Thanks, Mims.

Introduction

It is generally agreed by observers of United States manufacturing companies that many of our companies have lost and continue to lose market share to foreign competition. One major cause of this loss in market share is outmoded manufacturing methods. Some indicators of outmoded manufacturing methods within a plant are

- Unnecessarily long times between order placement and order shipment.

- Repeatedly missed delivery dates. This results in excessive past due shipping schedules to customers, and, consequently, lost sales.

- Excessive requests to customers for deviations from dimensional, metallurgical, or other specifications.

- Large amounts of scrap and rework of parts.

- A higher percentage of shipments in the last half of the month than in the first half (more than 2 to 1 in many cases).

- Bloated work in process inventories.

Many formulas have been advanced by various articles and books to overcome deficiencies in our approach to managing manufacturing companies. Most of these books describe a variety of concepts emphasizing or requiring quality improvements, potentially resulting in lower costs, improved deliveries, and shorter manufacturing lead times.

Some of the concepts related to improvement are

- *Just-in-time* inventory control, in which small amounts of inventory (ideally matching only the quantity ordered) are provided at various manufacturing stations just in time for processing. By minimizing inventory throughout the manufacturing pipelines, including those between suppliers and customers, the company forces efficiency and can detect and solve these uncovered problems.

- *Synchronous manufacturing* emphasizing carefully balanced continuous product flow with minimal delay and in-process inventories between manufacturing operations.

- The *flow of river* concept, emphasizing that lower in-process inventory uncovers problems that prevent the smooth flow of materials between manufacturing operations.

- Identifying *root causes* that prevent or minimize improvements (for example, capacity limitations, machinery breakdowns, vendor material quality deficiencies, and so on).

- Various scheduling procedures, like *Kanban* or *drum-buffer-rope,* which provides time buffers for unforeseen delays.

- Worker involvement, respect, and responsibility for solving problems.

- Minimizing batch sizes in production runs.

- Minimizing equipment setup times.

- Strong leadership, particularly from the chief executive.

- Employee training.

- Supplier performance evaluation and certification programs.

- Employing the benchmarking methods of the best companies.

- Reengineering the organization by reevaluating work requirements and methods.

- Organizing a plant into small integrated units within the same facility.

Several articles point out that many of these concepts have not achieved expected results. One article in the *Wall Street Journal* reaches several conclusions.[1]

- Concepts losing favor at some companies are heavy automation, quality circles, and just-in-time inventory systems.

- Companies have been obsessed with one fad or another at the cost of their overall focus.

- Companies that have found success by imitating the Japanese methods are in the minority.

- Most manufacturers are not improving fast enough compared to the competition.

Another article in the *Washington Post* concludes that many companies have seen little change in their earnings reports. It refers to a 1991 survey of 300 electronics companies that found that 73 percent of the companies had quality programs in place, but, of these, 63 percent said they had failed to improve quality by even as much as 10 percent.[2]

Hammer and Champy reach a similar conclusion about reengineering efforts, estimating that as many as 50 to 70 percent of the organizations that undertake a reengineering effort do not achieve the dramatic results they intended.[3]

Something is missing.

In this book I address some of the missing things.

Two major flaws exist in companies that are less than successful in achieving adequate results from manufacturing continuous improvement efforts.

1. Failure to include major *causal elements* contributing to major improvement into a total process.

2. Failure of leadership at the top of the organization to effectively implement such a total process.

Elements of a Total Process of Continuous Improvement

Throughout my career I have tried various methods to improve quality and reduce costs. Some worked well, some not so well, and some not at all. However, even when results were good, many times they didn't last. After many years of frustrating attempts to find the right formula for consistent and lasting quality and cost reduction, I have identified major causal elements that I feel are necessary to gain and hold significant improvements in those goals. Consistent application of these elements individually can improve results. However, the best results are achieved by integrating the elements into a total process. It is useful to think of the individual elements as necessary, but not sufficient, conditions for maximum improvement. *The right elements included in a total process, plus the right leadership, provide the sufficient conditions for significant continuous improvement.*

The Failure of Leadership

Volumes have been written on leadership in business organizations. Lately we've heard a lot about the leader's responsibility to provide a vision for the organization. I'm sure a vision can be extremely useful, when properly defined. The type of leadership I have found necessary to achieve, hold, and continuously improve manufacturing results is day-to-day observation by leaders (including the CEO) of an organization of what is really going on (auditing) with quality, delivery, lead time, and cost continuous improvement efforts, as well as detailed demonstration and coaching about what is expected.

It is the leaders' responsibility to define the process of continuous improvement—what the employees should do and how they should do it. But where leaders have failed in many organizations is that they do not spend the time (yes, on the plant floors, not in their offices) observing employees' quality of implementation and showing them the difference between what they are doing and what they should be doing. These are not responsibilities that should be delegated primarily to middle managers or consultants. Top managers should view consultants as *assisting* them in their responsibility to implement continuous improvement throughout their organizations. Proponents of the viewpoint that all one has to do is define the vision and employees will implement it on their own, with little direction, are kidding themselves.

In this book I describe a continuous improvement manufacturing process from an operating top management viewpoint, emphasizing how to construct and implement a continuous improvement method incorporating the basic management concepts of planning, organizing, directing/coaching, and controlling.

An operating management viewpoint is used to bring more realism to the problems managers face and to the actions that are needed to really fix these problems. Most books on manufacturing continuous improvement have been written by academicians or technical people—consultants with backgrounds such as manufacturing engineering or quality assurance. It is difficult for academicians, consultants, or staff personnel, no matter how experienced or qualified, to know firsthand the operating pressures, time constraints, multiple demands, and frustrations placed upon operating managers. There is no experience quite like being held responsible and accountable for manufacturing performance, putting into place solutions that you are confident will fix problems, and yet failing multiple times to adequately improve results. Such failure develops realism in problem solving.

The overall continuous improvement manufacturing management approach described in this book is the result of trial and error attempts to improve manufacturing operations using my own ideas, the suggestions of fellow employees, and many of the latest ideas espoused by academicians and consultants over the years. I admit that many of my observations are based on knowledge gained through some successes but also on various frustrations and failures to achieve hoped-for manufacturing improvements.

In this book, real-world examples of various elements of problem solving are provided. Many business managers have long lamented the scarcity of such examples in business writings. Such examples should be useful in providing an understanding of continuous improvement.

In addition, CEOs have a unique perspective on manufacturing. They must look at the success of the overall company and the strategic role of manufacturing in that success. Thus, this book's broader view and treatment of such topics as

- The role of customer requirements in manufacturing improvement
- Finding and training the right people to solve problems
- The critical role of the CEO in manufacturing improvement
- Translating improvement in quality, delivery, and lead time into profit and cash flow improvement

Other concepts emphasized in the book are the following:

1. In many cases the culture in manufacturing plants results in casual or informal problem solving. Minimal motivation to improve and poor problem-solving disciplines and skills exist. Problems are worked on only when convenient, and minimal problem prioritization is done. Group responsibilities with vague accountability are the norm. Communication with employees as to the actions being taken

is minimal. An approach is needed to counteract these cultural problems. This book places significant emphasis on formalizing actions that must take place to fix root causes. These actions should be

- Written action statements
- Assigned responsibilities and due dates
- Visual displays in the plant and the departments responsible
- Reviews and progress audits by top management

Such formalization may not be necessary in some cases. However, it is more necessary in certain situations than in others.

- The plant problem-solving culture is quite informal, and poor problem-solving disciplines and skills exist.
- The plant is so large in area or in number of employees as to make informal communication difficult. Even in situations where the intention is to break up the plant into subplants to allow more informal problem solving as recommended by Harmon, months or years may be required to accomplish such a reorganization.[4] In the meantime, problem solving could benefit from more formalization.
- A large number of problems exist with many actions required to remedy problems. Some formalization may be required just to keep track of all the actions, timing, and responsibilities.
- Rigid communication barriers exist between the many functions within manufacturing. Formalizing can help break down these functional barriers.

Finally, perhaps the most important argument for such formalization and for emphasizing the measurement of improvement (see point 2 in the next paragraph) is the unfortunate but real tendency that organizations that make substantial manufacturing improvements tend to fall back very soon into old habits and find that performance either regresses or levels off. Formalization and measurement of improvement minimizes the chances of such regression or leveling.

2. Emphasis is placed on the measurement of improvement in meeting customer requirements and remedying the root causes of poor quality, late delivery, and long lead times. Most of the articles and books on ways to improve manufacturing do not recommend specific methods of measuring improvement, either in customer requirements or in the root causes that plague attempts to improve. Without such measurement, however, managers have inadequate feedback as to which actions are working (and to what degree) and which are not.

3. Measurable customer requirements of both external and internal customers are identified. Meeting customer requirements such as quality and delivery should be among the objectives of a manufacturing continuous improvement management process. By meeting and exceeding such customer requirements, a company can improve its market share and strengthen its strategic position. Care should be taken not only to identify those requirements that customers feel are most important but also to develop methods to precisely measure the degree to which those requirements are met. If meeting external customer requirements is to improve, improvement must take place in various departments throughout the plant. In addition to satisfying the external customer requirements, emphasis is placed on defining and measuring improvement toward meeting requirements among internal departments.

The process described in this book has worked for me. It is capable of achieving significant improvement in manufacturing operations. Many authors state that results from a continuous improvement manufacturing process takes three to five years or more to realize. I disagree. Properly constructed and implemented, significant results can be realized within one to two years, depending on a company's culture and its employee experience base. However, it is not the latest fad in that it requires consistently hard work and dedication, particularly by top management. It should not be delegated to a consultant or lower echelon employee without heavy involvement and taking ownership by top management, particularly the CEO.

In summary, the goals of this book are

1. To describe the necessary causal elements of a continuous improvement manufacturing management process that, when implemented with the total process and with extensive leadership by top management, become the sufficient conditions for significant quality, delivery, lead time, and cost continuous improvement within one to two years

2. To provide real-world examples from my business experience (including various mistakes) that led to these recommendations

3. To suggest effective and efficient ways of translating the improvement of quality, delivery, and lead time into market share, profit, and cash flow improvement

A few words are necessary regarding what this book does not attempt to do.

1. Little attempt is made to extensively discuss subjects already covered in depth in existing literature such as just-in-time, benchmarking, or reengineering.

2. Nothing new is presented of a technical nature such as new concepts of experimentation or statistical measures of process control.

3. While the book adopts a CEO viewpoint toward continuous improvement, it does not discuss strategy or vision and how manufacturing should be part of such concepts. Much has already been written about these concepts of management and leadership. This book is written for those companies for which it already has been determined that improving manufacturing is important.

Certainly much has been written by others on what should be done to achieve continuous improvement, much of it theoretical. By using the words *actual experiences* in the title, I am limiting the scope of this book to how to make continuous improvement really work based on what has and what has not worked for me.

This book is written primarily for CEOs and top management as a practical "how to" guide for improving their businesses. Also, it can be helpful to continuous improvement teams of plant supervisory and staff diagnostic personnel by relating what approaches have succeeded and failed in my career. Finally, I would hope teachers and students would find the examples useful in providing a flavor of what actually goes on and what should go on in manufacturing.

A final note is that while most of my experiences are related to metalworking companies, the concepts recommended for achieving successful continuous improvement should also apply to other industries and manufacturing processes, because they are based on management principles applicable to most industries.

Notes

1. Amal Kumar Naj, "Shifting Gears: Some Manufacturers Drop Efforts to Adopt Japanese Techniques," *Wall Street Journal,* May 7, 1993, 1.

2. Jay Mathews, "Totaled Quality Management," *Washington Post,* June 6, 1993, H1 and H16.

3. Michael Hammer and James Champy, *Reengineering the Corporation* (New York: Harper Collins, 1993), 200.

4. Roy L. Harmon, *Reinventing the Factory* (New York: Free Press, 1990), 12–35.

Chapter 1

A Continuous Improvement Manufacturing Management Process To Meet Customer Requirements—Overview

This chapter suggests that manufacturing as a discipline within many U.S. companies received insufficient attention from top management during the 1970s and early 1980s. It proposes several reasons for that inattention and provides several examples. An overview of the process elements (continuous improvement manufacturing management process—CIMMP) recommended to achieve successful manufacturing continuous improvement is presented.

A New Role for Manufacturing

Examples abound about how the United States has become noncompetitive on a global basis in automobiles, televisions, cameras, refrigerators, air conditioners, power tools, steel, and various other products. The Japanese are the competitors most often identified as having forced us to look at our deficiencies and face the fact that we must improve in order to survive. So what went wrong? Simply put, the Japanese have outdone the United States by emphasizing and dramatically improving manufacturing quality and productivity.

We all know, from personal experience with many of these products, that the Japanese products have been, in most cases, better than U.S. products. They last longer, have fewer defects, and perform better. At the same time, the Japanese have reduced their manufacturing costs to such low levels that, except for the effects of periodic currency fluctuations, they are able to sell these products at lower prices than their U.S. competitors can. They have accomplished these feats by emphasizing manufacturing improvement to a degree never dreamed of by U.S. companies until the last few years. Thus, it is clear that U.S. companies must make a commitment to dramatically emphasize manufacturing improvement.

However, it has been my experience with a variety of companies that most management teams, although willing to improve manufacturing, don't know how. Many of these companies are doing some things better but lack an overall comprehensive manufacturing management approach that will improve quality and costs significantly enough to allow them to be globally competitive. This is primarily due to the lack until recently of sufficient top management attention to the manufacturing function in the organization and the lack of sufficient manufacturing functional experience in the backgrounds of top management in many U.S. companies. Hence, the tremendous growth of consulting companies selling approaches to manufacturing quality improvements and cost reduction, as well as the proliferation of books on the same subjects. Top managers are desperately searching for ways to install a quality and cost reduction process that works significantly, consistently, and for the long term. However, there are real pitfalls to relying exclusively on outsiders to provide the answers, particularly because most have minimal manufacturing operating experience.[1] More on this topic is discussed in chapter 7.

In most books on management and business for executives and business students published in the United States since 1960, the material covering manufacturing quality improvement and cost reduction in any depth is embarrassingly limited. The same goes for business school curricula. Figure 1.1 depicts the functional departments necessary to managing a business. The relative emphasis given to each department depends on the nature of a business's product and markets. However, it is probably safe to conclude that the function of

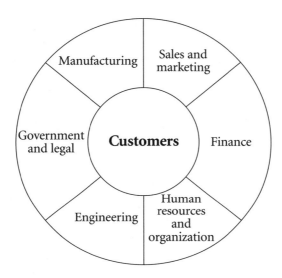

Figure 1.1. Typical functional departments in management.

manufacturing as a key strategic element has been sorely neglected. It seems that much attention has been devoted to developing the right product, at the right price, through the right channels of distribution, and promoting and selling it in the proper manner to the appropriate market segments. But little attention has been paid to the actual manufacture of the product. Until the Japanese beat us up with their brilliant execution of manufacturing strategy, manufacturing itself was almost an afterthought for most U.S. companies.

The Heavy Truck Market Environment—Mid 1970s

My first exposure to the manufacturing function was in the mid-seventies with a series of manufacturing jobs in Rockwell International's Automotive Operations heavy truck axle plants. I was in my early thirties and had been educated and experienced in marketing. I had been asking Rockwell management for a career path to general management, and they had responded that I needed plant experience. So off I went to a series of manufacturing positions as materials manager, manufacturing manager, plant manager, and general plants manager for four different heavy truck axles plants in a period of six years. I had the distinct disadvantage (or, perhaps, the advantage) of having had no education, training, or experience in manufacturing. The heavy-duty truck market at that time was enjoying a set of conditions similar to what the automobile manufacturers enjoyed before the Japanese started gaining significant market share.

- The economy was robust.
- Truck sales were strong.
- The profits of both truck manufacturers and their suppliers were healthy.
- Trucking deregulation had not yet hit.
- Although, in general, quality was not particularly high, no competitor was much better than any other.

It is safe to conclude that relative to today's competitive global environment, the incentive to dramatically improve quality and productivity was not great. The operational environments of the plants reflected these conditions.

- Measurement emphasis was on monthly shipments, production, profits, scrap levels, labor efficiency, and tool usage. There were few measures of the quality delivered to the customer.
- While monthly reports were available detailing part number scrap and labor efficiency by department and by shift, inadequate root-cause analysis was performed.
- Actions to improve scrap, labor efficiency, and past-due customer deliveries tended to concentrate on symptoms rather than root causes.

- Group employee meetings were not consistently held. There was no discussion of monthly financial results with hourly employees.

- Setup time for large multiple station automated machining equipment was measured in number of shifts.

- Formal, written, periodic evaluation of vendors was minimal.

- Axle design engineering was performed with minimal or no input from manufacturing.

- Union relations (UAW and Steelworkers) were confrontational. (I distinctly remember many management discussions about why hourly employees would not work harder to improve labor efficiency and scrap. Management was convinced that hourly employees had pegged production levels.) Involving hourly employees in root-cause analysis discussions was minimal and sporadic.

- Batch sizes were large to "improve" labor efficiency.

We existed quite nicely with this system because we, our customers, and our competitors were making profits. Our manufacturing inefficiencies were passed on to our customers in the form of annual price increases roughly equal to the annual rate of inflation. These annual price increases were a way of life throughout the entire supplier-customer chain all the way to the truck buyer. This example is not meant to criticize Rockwell's Automotive Operations management. Entire industries were engaged in the same approach.

I left the axle division before heavy truck industry conditions forced a new way of life. The truck industry was deregulated, and foreign competitors such as Mercedes, Volvo, and Fiat bought truck companies. The margins of truck common carriers, truck owner-operators, truck manufacturers, and their suppliers were ruthlessly squeezed. Many companies went out of business, and the industry consolidated. These pressures forced a new emphasis on manufacturing quality and productivity.

The Automotive Market Environment—Early 1980s

My first real taste of having to dramatically reduce cost under pressure conditions began in 1979. I had moved over to the passenger car component side of Rockwell's Automotive Operations as group vice president. Throughout the 1970s, the automotive market environment for quality and productivity was similar to that for heavy-duty trucks—manufacturing inefficiencies resulting in annual price increases throughout the supplier and customer pipeline. But in late 1979, the U.S. market for automobiles collapsed and entered into a four-year recession. U.S. auto companies suffered record losses. At the same time, Japanese auto manufacturers were gaining market share rapidly by offering cars with better quality and lower prices. This resulted in extreme pressure on automotive supplier companies to dramatically improve quality and reduce costs. For example, Ford Motor Company was rejecting stainless steel wheel covers with the smallest scratches or minor dings, conditions it had previously accepted, forcing a pileup of wheel cover rejects at the wheel cover plant. Aluminum wheels with the slightest surface imperfection were being rejected by General Motors, causing a similar pile of rejects at the cast aluminum wheel plant. Such rejections were happening to most automotive suppliers across most product lines. A new quality standard had been set for automotive suppliers that would never return to its previous lower levels.

At the same time those new quality standards began to take hold, suppliers were substantially reducing prices in an effort to maintain volume in their plants in the face of drastically reduced industry volumes. This, of course, resulted in major losses. The era of annual automobile supplier price increases was basically over. Suppliers reduced costs by a variety of means.

- Consolidating plants and warehouses
- Finding new offshore suppliers

- Squeezing price reductions out of vendors by promising to increase the volume of their purchases
- Soliciting union wage concessions
- Investing in new equipment technology and automation

Also, mostly driven by auto manufacturing companies, some suppliers tried to reduce costs through quality improvements. Quality departments expanded and moved up in the hierarchy of the organization. Quality circles and other employee involvement methods were introduced. Some of these efforts resulted in improvement. A few companies showed substantial gains but still lagged behind their Japanese counterparts. Clearly, new approaches were required. Many of these approaches, for example, just-in-time and synchronous manufacturing, are mentioned in the Introduction. Some of them, including some *total process* approaches are described in Appendix A. I am summarizing these approaches in an appendix because they are covered in detail in the literature.

All of these suggestions for quality and cost improvement are original and worthwhile. However, they tend to be somewhat general and provide few details and examples of how to improve. When struggling to develop such a continuous improvement process during my years in plant manufacturing, I found that some practical ideas were either lacking or insufficiently implemented. These ideas include

- Making actual customer requirements the basis for manufacturing goals, and measuring the organization's progress toward meeting these goals
- Creating written action lists for all plant departments and assigning responsibility and timing targets
- Displaying these action lists and results for employees to see
- Reviews by top management of progress in meeting customer requirements, remedying root causes, and meeting actions

- Developing written departmental procedures for guiding ongoing actions
- Observing and coaching about what is supposed to be taking place in departments
- Describing what is required to adequately identify root causes
- Providing real-world examples of many of these concepts

There is a need for a comprehensive manufacturing problem-solving process that incorporates these ideas. The process recommended here is called a continuous improvement manufacturing management process (CIMMP). It is basically a process that identifies and removes obstacles to continuously improving quality, delivery, lead time, and costs, as well as conserving working capital.

Figure 1.2 depicts the recommended overall continuous improvement manufacturing management process.[2] The process begins with the task of identifying measurable, major customer requirements (Box 1). The major customer requirement examples discussed in this book are

- Product quality (conformance to specifications)
- On-time delivery
- Lead time, that is, the time an order is placed until it is ready to ship to the customer

Table 1.1 lists the specific measures used as examples for the general requirements of quality, delivery, and lead time.

Certainly other customer requirements can be used, depending on their importance to customers, but these have been chosen as examples. The customer requirements that a company decides to improve should be those that are very important to target customers and, preferably, those for which a competitive advantage can be gained.

As soon as a company has tentatively identified the measurable, major customer requirements, meetings should be held with customers

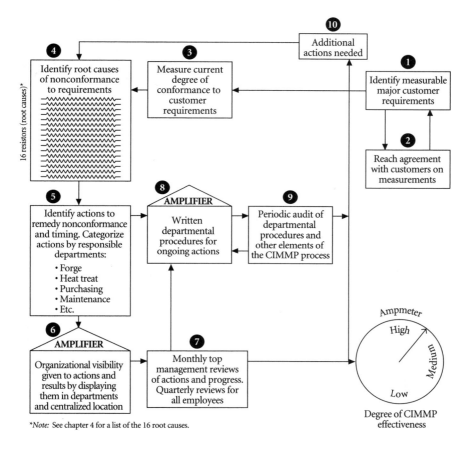

Figure 1.2. Continuous improvement manufacturing management process to meet customer requirements (depicted as an electric circuit).

to reach agreement on the specific requirements and how confor-mance to them will be measured (Box 2). In most cases, the tentative requirements determined by a supplier will be changed after these customer meetings, because customers are more knowledgeable about the subsequent use of the product.

Table 1.1. Measurable customer requirements.

General	Specific and Measurable
Quality	Key characteristic control chart and C_{pk} value Dimensional Metallurgical
Delivery	Percent of pieces shipped on time to an agreed upon schedule
Lead time	Number of days or weeks from order placement to shipment

When the supplier and customer have agreed on a set of requirements and measurements, the actual degree of conformance to the requirements (Box 3) must be measured. Feedback is needed regarding the effectiveness of actions to determine the resulting degree of improvement. A continuous improvement process without such measurements lacks a key element; without such measurement, management does not know whether the actions it is taking are resulting in improvement to customer requirements.

Chapter 2 discusses the subjects depicted by Boxes 1, 2, and 3.

Any conditions that do not conform to customer requirements require, first, a causal analysis. Chapter 3 discusses the root-cause analysis of nonconformance to customer requirements (Box 4). A root cause is that cause that is left when continuing to ask "why" yields no further useful information about how to eliminate the cause. Chapter 3 also discusses the use of teams and worker involvement in root-cause analysis. The following types of root causes are discussed in chapter 4.

- Inadequate process instructions
- Employees' failure to follow process instructions
- Equipment breakdown or incapability
- Tooling incapability or complexity
- Inefficient plant layout

- Inefficient process routing
- Inferior quality of vendor material, and/or untimely delivery
- Difficult or complex part design
- Inadequate operator and supervisor training and instruction
- Inadequate departmental support methods and paperwork
- Restrictive union contract provisions
- Equipment or operational bottlenecks
- Excessive setup time
- Excessive production batch sizes
- Employee concern for job security
- Inadequate employee rewards

Successfully determining root causes results in the identification of actions that will correct these root causes. Chapter 5 discusses the actions required to remedy the root causes of customer requirement nonconformance (Box 5), displaying the actions required and the results achieved in various departments (Box 6), the necessity of periodic progress meetings regarding actions and customer requirement results (Box 7), and written procedures for any actions necessary on an ongoing basis (Box 8). It is suggested the actions be categorized by organizational departments, that the names of those responsible for taking the actions are identified, and that timing targets be set. As soon as the actions are categorized by department, each department's own actions should be prominently displayed in those departments and in a central location so that employees can see a summary of all actions to be taken by the company. Results such as improvements in quality, delivery, lead time, and cost should also be displayed. This makes everyone in the organization aware of the progress toward improvements and what needs to be done to continually improve results. It also builds morale and provides a feeling of accomplishment. Periodic progress meetings reviewing departmental actions, responsibilities, and timing keep management up to date and let the entire organization know that management is interested and involved. These reviews can be conducted in the departments responsible for performing the actions, thus making the review process visible to department employees.

Some of the departmental actions required to achieve optimum customer requirements should be performed regularly. For example, all the individual pieces of tooling required to set up for a different part number on an NC lathe should be available at the lathe when the setup is scheduled. This prevents delays in starting the setup. Because this type of action should be done every time there is a setup, some method of formally communicating this to the organization is needed. Written departmental procedures accomplish this. Each department in a plant should develop and utilize written departmental procedures that represent those key actions that should be performed on an ongoing basis to achieve optimum results. Certainly, the objective is not to have a thick procedure manual that everyone ignores because it contains unnecessary and trivial procedures. Instead, the objective is to have a departmental manual of procedures that describe the important critical actions required to achieve consistent optimum results for a department. The judgment as to which procedures will be included should be made by each department manager with guidance from the prime driver of continuous improvement.

Chapter 6 discusses the need for leadership by top management: auditing, or observing, all elements of CIMMP, including auditing departmental procedures (Box 9) and demonstrating performance expectations. Human nature being what it is, someone needs to audit how well the organization is implementing all elements of the continuous improvement process. How performance expectations for all steps in the continuous improvement process are communicated and demonstrated is also covered. An organization that is not used to thinking in terms of continuous improvement will probably have relatively low standards of performance and a low sense of urgency. It is difficult to create a sufficiently high sense of urgency and superb standards of performance through formal classroom training. The most effective method is demonstration on the job by someone with both a high sense of urgency and high standards of performance. This minimizes the danger that problem solvers will take "easy answer" causes which are really symptoms rather than exercise the discipline and tenacity required to uncover root causes.

Chapter 6 also discusses the fact that a continuous improvement process always requires additional actions (Box 10). As more is learned about the degree of conformance to customer requirements and progress in remedying root causes, the need for new actions will be identified. This is because customer requirements will never be perfectly met if they are continually set higher once they are achieved. That is what the concept of continuous improvement is all about. The continuous improvement manufacturing management process is depicted as an electric circuit in Figure 1.2. For electricity to emerge at the end of the circuit, all parts of the circuit must be connected. Thus, Boxes 1–5, 7, and 9–10 must be in place if a continuous improvement undertaking is to be optimally effective. Boxes 6 and 8 (the written departmental procedures and the display of actions and results) are depicted as electric current amplifiers; they are not absolutely necessary, but they do serve to enhance an optimally effective continuous improvement process. Also, the 16 major root causes in Box 4 are shown as electric current resistors in that each will reduce the process effectiveness until they are remedied. The more the root causes are remedied, the less negative effect they will have on the process.

Chapter 7 discusses the role of the leader in financial improvement: translating improvements in quality, delivery, and lead time into profit and increased cash flow. As root causes are remedied, resulting in improved quality, delivery, and lead times, the potential develops for dramatically reduced costs and inventory. As the root causes are remedied, the speed at which materials move through the plant increases, because many of the obstacles have been removed. With this speed comes the need for less labor (plant direct, indirect, and salary) because there will be reduced scrap and rework and improved productivity. Material usage should also be reduced with lower scrap. And there will be a substantial reduction in work-in-process inventory (heretofore created by rework, rerunning scrap parts, parts deviations submitted to customers, and excessive process times). With closer vendor relations and partnership, raw materials inventory can be reduced by faster vendor response times. And less finished inventory need be carried to compensate for internal inefficiencies and missed customer delivery dates.

Notice the reference to the potential for dramatically reduced cost and inventory. As root causes are remedied, there will be a need for less labor. Either sales and production will have to be dramatically increased with the same labor, or labor will have to be reduced to obtain the cost reductions. Just as labor will not reduce itself, neither will inventories. These issues are also discussed in chapter 7, in addition to suggestions about the use of consultants.

Chapter 8 discusses the varying needs for formality in the continuous improvement process depending on a company's culture and other factors. It also presents some final observations.

Appendix A defines and describes selected popular manufacturing concepts such as just-in-time. Appendix B provides varied examples of departmental actions with assigned responsibilities and timing.

Notes

1. John A. Byrne, "Managing for Quality: Consultants—High Priests and Hucksters," *Business Week* Special Issue (October 25, 1991): 52–54.

2. For simplification, this process will be referred to throughout the remainder of this book as the continuous improvement process. Also, the examples used are for metal manufacturing companies. However, this continuous improvement process is sufficiently flexible to be adapted to other types of products and various industries.

Chapter 2

Customer Requirements

**Continuous Improvement Manufacturing Management
Process to Meet Customer Requirements
(depicted as an electric circuit)**

⑩ Additional actions needed

④ Identify root causes of nonconformance to requirements

16 resistors (root causes)*

③ Measure current degree of conformance to customer requirements

① Identify measurable major customer requirements

② Reach agreement with customers on measurements

⑤ Identify actions to remedy nonconformance and timing. Categorize actions by responsible departments:
- Forge
- Heat treat
- Purchasing
- Maintenance
- Etc.

⑧ AMPLIFIER
Written departmental procedures for ongoing actions

⑨ Periodic audit of departmental procedures and other elements of the CIMMP process

⑥ AMPLIFIER
Organizational visibility given to actions and results by displaying them in departments and centralized location

⑦ Monthly top management reviews of actions and progress. Quarterly reviews for all employees

Ampmeter
High
Medium
Low

Degree of CIMMP effectiveness

*Note: See chapter 4 for a list of the 16 root causes.

This chapter covers the three elements involved in satisfying customer requirements.

1. Identifying measurable, major customer requirements (Box 1)
2. Reaching agreement with customers on what their major requirements are (Box 2)
3. Measuring the degree of conformance to those requirements (Box 3)

Several examples demonstrate the need for these elements.

• At one company we had been using final inspection dimensional layout and sonic inspection for porosity as the basic quality measurements supplied to a major customer. When we asked the customer's representatives whether these were adequate measures of quality, they told us that one of our competitors had been providing them the data they really needed. These were in-process measurements in addition to final dimensional and metallurgical measurements, and C_{pk} values (more about these later). A competitor had gained an advantage, and we didn't know about it because we hadn't asked.

• The same company had been supplying another customer with a partially machined part. We had been supplying them with inspection measurements on five dimensions for years. When we asked them if they required any other quality information, they added two more dimensions that were key locating points for their final machining operations. When we began controlling these two new dimensions, their cost of machining these locating points was reduced. We ended up sharing in some of these savings.

• In separate plastic wheel cover and wire wheel cover assembly operations, we had great difficulty meeting delivery deadlines to Ford Motor Company. In an attempt to improve on-time deliveries, we did several things that we were convinced would work. We added workers to speed up assembly time, we increased inventories of purchased parts used in assemblies, and we added more lead time to our vendor schedules.

We were relying on Ford to tell us whether the timeliness of our deliveries was improving, because we had no definitive measurements of our own. But it took us months to discover that a major cause of our delivery problems was the fact that parts we were purchasing (for example, fasteners, plastic logos) from many small vendors were being delivered late to us because of our vendors' own internal quality problems. We had assumed that, because we were taking multiple actions, improvements would result. Had we had our own measurements of the degree to which we were meeting Ford's delivery schedules, we would have recognized our lack of progress earlier. We installed a weekly measurement by part number of the percentage of schedule shipped on time to Ford. That percentage increased eventually from 50 percent to 96 percent as we resolved the root causes of late delivery.

• At another company we had a large scrap and rework problem. We identified the 10 part numbers with the largest dollar scrap for the prior 12 months and assigned a quality department team to identify the root causes of scrap and rework for those 10 part numbers. The team developed a list of root causes and the actions that were being taken to lower scrap and rework rates. We even had a "war room" on the walls of which these actions were posted. For these 10 part numbers, we must have had 30 actions to be taken by five different departments. What we did not do was develop a timely quantitative measurement of our progress in reducing scrap and rework for these 10 part numbers every time they were produced. When we finally developed such measures, we found out that despite all the actions we were taking, there was minimal improvement on scrap and rework. After assigning cross-functional problem-solving teams to identify the root causes, we reduced scrap and rework by half. We probably wasted a year by not having quantitative measures of improvement early when we started taking actions we thought would lead to improvement.

Identifying Measurable Major Customer Requirements (Box 1)

Because of the extreme importance of accurately measuring customer requirements, detailed examples of these measurements are provided. Three customer requirements have been chosen as examples: quality, delivery, and lead time (how fast a customer can place an order and receive delivery). These three requirements have been extremely important to most of the customers that I have sold to throughout my career. The actual customer requirements chosen for any given company, however, should be chosen for strategic reasons. The customer requirements that a company chooses to improve and measure must be important enough to customers that they favor a supplier who gains a competitive advantage on those requirements. Also, a company should choose customer requirements on which it is both willing and able to achieve a competitive advantage. It may be that a company lacks the money to make the improvements necessary on some customer requirements without recapitalizing. In addition, competitors may be so strong in some customer requirements that improving other customer requirements where a company can gain a competitive advantage would be more fruitful.

Table 1.1 on page 10 depicts quality, delivery, and lead time as customer requirements. It also shows how more general requirements can be stated in specific, measurable terms (Box 1).

Measuring Conformance to Customer Requirements (Box 3)

Quality

Whatever measurements are used for quality, they should be chosen for the degree to which they represent the aspects of quality required by the supplier's customers. The quality measurement example used here is for a company providing internal jet engine forgings to jet engine manufacturers such as General Electric, Pratt & Whitney, and Rolls Royce. Because quality requirements are so strict for such parts, measurement requirements are quite stringent. We will go into significant detail in this example to demonstrate what is sometimes required, and also because these quality measurement concepts have gained favor recently in some quality programs in industry. To repeat, the quality measurements described here are used by a supplier because *its customers want it done this way.* Much simpler measures of quality such as the number of customer returns or the percentage of rejects at final inspection can be used if they are acceptable to customers and measure true improvements in quality and associated costs.

The measurements used for quality in this example will be termed key characteristics, both dimensional and metallurgical. *Key characteristics* are defined as those product features that have the greatest influence upon the product fit, performance, or service life. Examples are metal tensile strength; metal hardness; and dimensions of height, width, length, and weight. Figure 2.1 shows a cross section of a jet engine turbine disc forging. The key characteristics shown in Figure 2.2 relate to the shaded area of the disc in Figure 2.1. Figure 2.2 shows key characteristics as follows:

- In-process characteristics of the rough metal stock prior to the forging operation.

  1. Outer faces should be parallel within .015 inch.

  2. Locator hole should be concentric within .015 inch.

  3. Weight as machined should be 90.4 pounds plus or minus 1 pound.

- In-process characteristics of the rough forging after forging but prior to machining.

  1. The depth of the depression should be .5 inch plus or minus .08 inch.

  2. The distance at one location of the disc should be 1.8 inches plus or minus .08 inch.

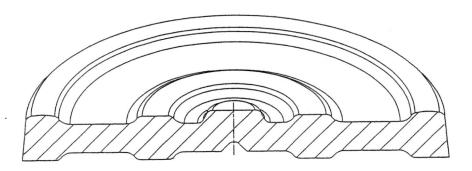

Figure 2.1. Cross section of a jet engine turbine disc.

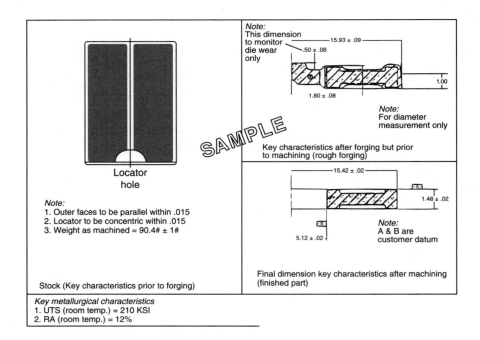

Figure 2.2. Key characteristics of a jet engine turbine disc.

3. The distance from the disc center to the outside point should be 15.93 inches plus or minus .09 inch.

4. The distance from the center of the outside point to the bottom point should be 1 inch.

- Final dimension characteristics of the finished forging after machining.

  1. The distance from the disc center to the beginning edge of the shoulder should be 5.12 inches plus or minus .02 inch.

  2. The distance from the disc center to the outside point should be 15.42 inches plus or minus .02 inch.

  3. The height of the disc at its outer point should be 1.48 inches plus or minus .02 inch.

- Final metallurgical characteristics of the finished forging.

  1. Ultimate tensile strength at room temperature should be a minimum of 210,000 pounds per square inch.

  2. Reduction of area at room temperature should be a minimum of 12 percent.

It is imperative that key quality characteristics are easily measurable as are those just discussed. Thus improvement, or lack thereof, is readily determined. Since it is not practical to measure all possible dimensional and metallurgical characteristics because of time and cost constraints, it is important that the product characteristics chosen as key are the ones that reflect the greatest influence on the product quality *as defined by customers.*

To the extent that any of the characteristics chosen as key do not reflect the greatest influence on product quality (or that characteristics influencing product quality are not chosen, and thus not measured), there is risk that product of insufficient quality may be shipped to customers. It is very important to spend the time and effort to identify and verify that the characteristics chosen as key are those that are most predictive of product fit, performance, or service life.

To prevent quality problems most effectively, key characteristics should be developed and production runs measured for all part numbers.

In the following example, the method required by customers for measuring actual key characteristics against target values is twofold. Each key characteristic for each part number requires a control chart and a C_{pk} value.

Figure 2.3 depicts a control chart for a target weight. The chart contains 25 individual weight measurements plotted as to their actual weights. The chart has an upper and lower limit corresponding to the target control limits of 98 and 102 pounds (100 pounds plus or minus 2 pounds). In this example, all 25 weights are within the target control limits and are fairly well centered (low variation) in that the range of weights is between 99.4 and 100.8 pounds.

The more centered and narrow the variation, the more consistent a part will be in its fit, performance, and service life. Therefore, it is beneficial to have a measure of the amount of variation and centeredness around the target value. This measure of centeredness and variability is called a C_{pk} value.

Reviewing monthly trend summaries of control chart and C_{pk} values for various part numbers will provide a monitor of the improvement in quality over time. Relevant summary statistics to track might be

- The percentage of parts run within control limits for a key characteristic for a part number

- The percentage of parts run within control limits for all key characteristics for a part number

- The percentage of parts run within control limits for all key characteristics for all part numbers

Part no. – Rel. no.		Cut weight—target	Control limits		
XXXX-XX		100.0 pounds	± 2%		
Part name					

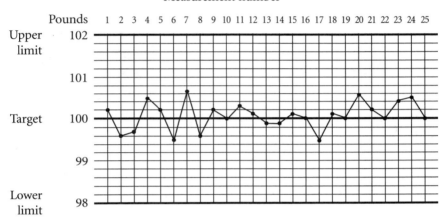

Figure 2.3. Cut weight control chart.

- The percentage of parts run meeting a target C_{pk} value for various key characteristics for various part numbers

Delivery

As shown in Table 1.1 on page 10, the measurement used for delivery in this example is the percentage of pieces of a given part number for a given order quantity that is shipped on time to an agreed upon schedule. (This measure assumes the customer arranges for the transportation carrier. If the supplier arranges for the carrier and is responsible for delivery to the customer's location, the measure should be the quantity received on time by the customer.) Many times a customer will request delivery of a part with insufficient lead time. While every attempt should be made by the supplier to meet this early date, this is not the only date for which the supplier should measure its performance on delivery. The appropriate date against which to measure on-time delivery is one negotiated between the customer (the date required) and the supplier, taking into consideration the supplier's material lead times and processing times.

Table 2.1 shows a delivery performance analysis report for various part numbers. The percentage of pieces shipped on time to an agreed upon schedule gives a clear picture of delivery performance for a period of time. Again, reviewing this percentage monthly, in various summary forms, allows the supplier to monitor improvement in delivery.

Lead Time

As shown in Table 1.1, the measurement used for lead time in this example is the number of days from order placement to actual readiness to ship (including complete paper and test documentation) of the number of parts ordered. Some care should be taken in defining *order placement* and *readiness to ship.* In many situations, the date of order placement can be fuzzy. Figure 2.4 depicts some major activities that might take place prior to product shipment. These activities,

Table 2.1. Delivery performance analysis report.

Part number	Delivery schedule agreed to	Total quantity ordered	Quantity shipped on time	Balance due	Percent shipped on time	Percent balance due
175	05-01-91	11	8	3	73	27
176	05-13-91	45	1	44	2	98
177	03-18-91	54	47	7	87	13
178	04-19-91	5	2	3	40	60
178	06-13-91	8	5	3	63	37
178	07-19-91	4	4	0	100	0
178	08-16-91	7	1	6	14	86
180	10-12-90	22	22	0	100	0

Customer Order Processing

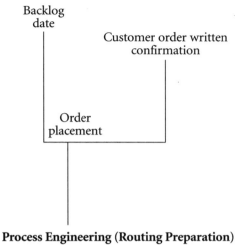

Process Engineering (Routing Preparation)

Raw Material Procurement

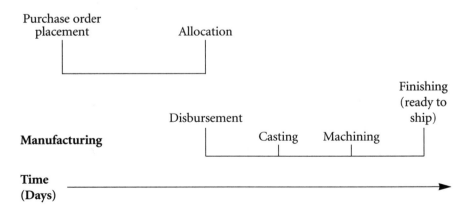

Figure 2.4. Customer requirements—Lead time: Days required to complete work of various departments.

some taking place concurrently, are customer order processing, process engineering (routing preparation), procurement of raw materials, and manufacturing.

The order placement date is defined by the sales order entry person. He or she makes that designation when there is confidence that the customer really will accept delivery of the parts ordered. The backlog date shown is the date the customer calls to verbally place the order. The sales order entry person does not define that date as the order placement date because many times changes in the type and quantity of parts are made before written confirmation is received from the customer. In fact, several weeks or more can elapse before written confirmation is received. The ready to ship date must also be precisely defined if the lead time measurement is to be consistent. Basically, the ready to ship date should be the date that all supplier requirements are complete and the potential control passes to the customer. Thus, if the parts are packed in the shipping area and waiting for customer-arranged transportation or inspection, they are counted as ready to ship. (As with the delivery measure, if the supplier is responsible for delivery to the customer, the lead time measured should end when the parts are received by the customer.) Monthly reviews of the actual number of days of lead time by part number, customer averages, product grouping averages, or total company average allow conclusions to be drawn about improvement in lead time.

Internal Customers

The discussion thus far has emphasized three important external customer requirements and their measurement. That is, we have been talking about the supplier's external customer. To increase the probability of meeting, or making improvement toward meeting, external customer requirements, it is recommended for some companies that the concept of internal customer requirements also be used.

This concept requires that major, measurable, internal customer requirements be developed for most departments within the supplier company. In other words, if quality of work and timing of output is defined and measured for each individual department and if corrections to problems are completed, the result will be continuous improvement in meeting the external customer's requirements as well. In fact, one wonders how continuous improvement could be accomplished for the external customer if it is not accomplished within the supplier firm's individual departments. And for the same reasons that it is necessary to measure how well a company meets the external customer's requirements, in most cases it is also necessary to measure progress in improving internal department requirements.

Table 2.2 depicts an example of internal supplier/customer relationships for one company. It can be seen that the heat treat department can be both a supplier and a customer.

Table 2.3 shows an example of the heat treat department as a customer and the quality metallurgical department as a supplier to the heat treat department. The measurable requirements of the heat treat department are the following:

- At least 90 percent of the time, the load cards should arrive in heat treat 48 hours before the castings arrive.

- When received in heat treat, the load cards should be completed and legible 100 percent of the time.

- When heat–treat related metallurgical property failures occur, computer data should be updated and heat treat notified within one day of failure 100 percent of the time.

Table 2.4 shows the measurement of the actual performance over time of the quality metallurgy department in meeting the requirements of the heat treat department.

Table 2.2. Heat treat department supplier/customer relationships.

Suppliers ⟶	Heat Treat ⟶ Department	Customers
Production control		Production control
Quality–metallurgy		Quality–metallurgy
Die room		Die room
Inspection		Inspection
Processing		Processing
Foundry (casting)		Production machine
Production machine		Microstructure control
Quality–dimensional		Accounting
Physical test		
Documentation and records		

Table 2.3. Supplier/customer agreement.

Supplier:	Quality metallurgy	
Customer:	Heat treat	
Product(s):	Load cards/procedures	
Product attribute requirements	**Quality**	**Delivery**
1. Load card should arrive in heat treat department.	90%	48 hours before castings arrive
2. Load cards should be legible and complete.	100%	As received in heat treat
3. Update computer data and notify heat treat when heat treat–related failures occur.	100%	Within one day of metallurgical property failure
Supplier date:		Customer:
Date:		

Table 2.4. Supplier/customer agreement: Requirements performance.

Supplier:	Quality metallurgy						
Customer:	Heat treat						
Product(s):	Load cards/procedures						
	Target Percent of Time	**Actual Percent of Time**					
Requirement		Jan	Feb	Mar	Apr	May	June
1. Load card should arrive in heat treat department 48 hours before castings arrive.	90	65	67	70	70	75	80
2. Load cards should be							
• Legible	100	78	85	90	90	92	94
• Complete	100	75	83	87	94	96	96
3. Update computer data and notify heat treat within one day of failure when heat treat metallurgical property failures occur.	100	60	65	75	85	88	88

Reaching Agreements with External and Internal Customers (Box 2)

In reaching a final set of definitions of a customer's measurable requirements, it is imperative that a customer has input to these requirements and agrees with the final version. Since customers know best the use to which they will put a supplier's parts, they are in the best position to define their own requirements. For example, one customer may further machine a part received from a supplier. The customer may have a numerically controlled lathe that uses target positions to locate the part on the lathe prior to machining. Normally, a supplier would not know about the critical nature of those machining locator points unless they were identified on the part print.

Another reason for obtaining customer agreement on requirement definitions is that if customers are involved up front, they are more likely to accept actual results when presented. Also it is likely that, as both suppliers and customers gain experience with the measurement data on requirements, changes to those requirements will occur.

This chapter covered the customer requirement portion (Boxes 1–3) of the continuous improvement manufacturing management process described in chapter 1. The next chapter describes the methods used to identify and evaluate the root causes of nonconformance to customer requirements, and selected organizational issues (Box 4).

Chapter 3

Root Cause Analysis of Nonconformance to Customer Requirements

**Continuous Improvement Manufacturing Management
Process to Meet Customer Requirements
(depicted as an electric circuit)**

④ Identify root causes of nonconformance to requirements

16 resistors (root causes)*

③ Measure current degree of conformance to customer requirements

⑩ Additional actions needed

① Identify measurable major customer requirements

② Reach agreement with customers on measurements

⑤ Identify actions to remedy nonconformance and timing. Categorize actions by responsible departments:
• Forge
• Heat treat
• Purchasing
• Maintenance
• Etc.

⑧ AMPLIFIER Written departmental procedures for ongoing actions

⑨ Periodic audit of departmental procedures and other elements of the CIMMP process

⑥ AMPLIFIER Organizational visibility given to actions and results by displaying them in departments and centralized location

⑦ Monthly top management reviews of actions and progress. Quarterly reviews for all employees

Ampmeter
High
Medium
Low
Degree of CIMMP effectiveness

*Note: See chapter 4 for a list of the 16 root causes.

In chapter 2, customer requirements were identified and measured as to their degree of conformance. When quality, delivery, or lead time requirements are not being met, root-cause analysis is required. Root-cause analysis and methods are discussed in this chapter along with selected observations on organizing for root-cause analysis (Box 4).

Root-Cause Analysis

A *root cause* is defined as the cause that is left when continuing to ask "why" does not yield any more useful information for eliminating the cause. Root-cause analysis is not easy. Take the example of a forging order being late for customer delivery. Initial investigation of the cause determined that the die in the forging hammer broke. Further causal analysis centered on the quality of the die. It was determined that the die had been manufactured to print and that the print design was correct. Even further investigation revealed that the die was set up improperly in the forging hammer. But why was it set up improperly? The operator who usually sets up this job was off sick when the job was set up. A substitute operator set up the job, following the written instructions for the setup, but made an error in that the die was three inches higher than it was supposed to be. The root cause appears to be that an inexperienced substitute setup operator was allowed to set up the job and that final checking of the setup by, for example, the operator's supervisor was inadequate.

In another example, 100 percent of a production run of large forgings was undersized. It was first thought that the die was under-sized, but the die checked good to print. Then investigators checked the weight of the metal charge going into the die. It was correct. The cause was traced to the fact that the metal in the die prior to hammering was too cold to fill out to the proper size. But why? Furnace temperatures were checked. They were up to proper temperature. Next, it was determined that the lift truck driver was taking too long to transfer the forgings from the furnace to the die. The written instructions detailed the proper time and method of transfer, so why was the driver taking so long? Finally, it was revealed that the truck driver had just transferred from another department and was assigned to the job without proper instruction from the supervisor. This was the real root cause.

In a third example, a job was late to the customer because the metal vendor was late in delivering the metal to the manufacturer. Investigation determined that the manufacturer's purchasing department ordered the material late. Why? The manufacturer's engineering department was late in getting the metal specification to purchasing. Why? The manufacturer's sales order department had made a late change to the metal specification and had directed purchasing to hold the metal order. Why? The real root cause: The customer had held up the order because it had made a late change to the metal specification; the sales order department probably should have rescheduled the delivery for a later date.

These examples show that root-cause analysis can be complicated and that patience and tenacity are required to come up with the actual root cause.

Root-Cause Analysis Methods

A variety of authors have written about many methods used for root-cause analysis. Juran and Gryna divide the methods into those used in the study of symptoms, those used to theorize about causes, and those used for data collection and analysis.[1] The methods discussed are shown in Table 3.1.

Scholtes also describes the methods used for root-cause analysis in a chapter entitled "Tools of the Scientific Approach."[2]

Methods described are

- Flowcharts
- Pareto charts

Table 3.1. Methods used for root-cause analysis.

Phase of Diagnosis	Technique
Study of symptoms	Check sheet
	Autopsies
	Glossary
	Pareto analysis
Theorizing about causes	Brainstorming
	Nominal group technique
	Storyboarding
	Tabular arrangement
	Cause-and-effect diagram
	Force-field analysis
	Affinity diagram
	Structure fee
	Why–why diagram
	Interrelationship digraph
	Program decision process chart
	Matrix
	Check sheet
	Pareto analysis
Data collection and analysis	Historical review
	Check sheet
	Pareto analysis
	Flow diagram
	Arrow diagram
	Process capability analysis
	Stream-to-stream analysis
	Time-to-time analysis
	Cumulative data plots
	Probability paper
	Control charts
	Piece-to-piece analysis
	Within piece-to-piece analysis
	Multi-vari diagram
	Defect concentration diagram
	Interrelation of variables
	Correlation
	Ranking
	Matrix
	Measurements at intermediate stages
	Measurements following noncontrolled operations
	Measurement of additional properties
	Study of worker methods
	Formal experiments
	Other statistical techniques
	Measurements for diagnosis

Source: J. M. Juran, ed., *Juran's Quality Control Handbook,* 4th ed. (New York: McGraw-Hill, 1988), 22.33–34.

- Cause-and-effect diagrams
- Stratification and is/is not analysis
- Time plots
- Control charts
- Dot plots and stem-and-leaf displays
- Checksheets
- Scatter diagrams[2]

Because a detailed description of these methods is provided in these two books and by various other authors, I will not cover them here. My intent is to discuss the human element and management issues related to root-cause analysis rather than the technical methods involved.

Some comment, however, is required on the danger of excessive data collection and analysis. The sheer number of techniques available for root-cause analysis may encourage their overuse. I have seen a situation where a large, complex part had a high level of scrap, rework, and submittals to the customer for dimension deviations every time the part was run. The parts were not filling out the dies and too often were undersized, but at different locations of the part. This condition lasted over a period of almost a year, and new batches of the part were being run continuously to keep up with customer schedule requirements. The company was losing a lot of money on this part (the selling price was more than $15,000) due to the high levels of scrap and rework, the extra air freight charges, and the low labor productivity. Process engineers had been collecting data for months on the correlation of experimental results to different heat treat furnace temperatures, and on several other potential causal variables. Finally, during a meeting of departmental supervisors and operators, an operator suggested adding 40 pounds of metal to the starting metal charge. Process engineering resisted this because it had spent time reducing the weight in order to lower costs. However, it was decided to try adding the 40 pounds of weight (at about $1 per pound, it amounted to less than 1 percent of the selling price), and the job has run consistently well ever since.

The point to be made is that, many times, getting people with the right experience and knowledge of equipment and tooling together (including operators), and trying a few commonsense actions, can substitute for weeks and months of data collection and analysis.

Another example relates to a heavy truck rear axle assembly plant. A two-month study was being conducted on the multiple reasons that axle shipments were late. Past-due schedules were high, and inventories were excessive. A process engineering group cataloged and correlated the number of days late to the various part numbers and causes. A group meeting was held with various departments, including component part manufacturing personnel and hourly assembly workers. After two hours of discussion, it was concluded that the sales order department was scheduling the assembly plant beyond the capability of the suppliers. This happened to be occurring during a period of excessive short-term demand, so it made little sense to try to expand supply capabilities to match the increased plant sales schedules. Instead, sales schedules were cut back to more closely match supply capabilities. Customers received more reliable shipping promises, and inventories were reduced. There is a place for data collection and analysis, but care must be taken not to overuse these tools, particularly in place of good logical analysis by experienced employees knowledgeable in plant operations, products, and processes.

Actions Required to Remedy Root Causes

The better the investigation into finding the root causes of nonconformance to customer requirements, the better the quality of information that is gathered with which the actions necessary to remedy the causes can be identified. In the first example given in the section,

Root-Cause Analysis, on page 32, the root cause was that an inexperienced operator was allowed to set up the job with inadequate supervision and final checking. An action that should remedy this root cause might be a written departmental procedure that requires a defined second party to measure the setup parameters any time someone other than the main setup person sets up the job.

In the second example, the root cause was that a new truck driver was not given proper instruction by the supervisor. The action to remedy the root cause should be that all employees assigned to transfer parts from furnaces to dies be given written instructions and training as to how much time is allowed for such transfers. An additional action might be that, after such instruction, the supervisor observe the newly assigned employee executing transfers until he or she is satisfied the employee is able to execute the procedures correctly and consistently.

In the third example, the root cause was that the customer had held up the order due to a late change in specifications. The action could be that delivery promise dates be rescheduled any time customer actions are likely to cause original delivery promise dates to be missed.

To the extent that causes described are still just symptoms and not root causes, the actions recommended to be taken are not as likely to remedy the real problem. Actions to remedy root causes will be further discussed in chapter 5.

Organization for Root-Cause Analysis

The search for a problem's root cause can be extremely frustrating for a number of reasons including the following four.

1. *The temptation to conclude that a symptom is the root or real cause is great.* It takes time, patience, and tenacity to progress through a series of *whys* to get to the root cause. It is easier to settle on seemingly obvious answers rather than spend the time and effort to dig deeper.

2. *Many organizations are resistant to change.* Getting people to cooperate during the search for root causes may be difficult. How they are asked or required to be involved is critical. At one investment casting manufacturing company, plant supervisors and hourly personnel asked if I could get the process engineers to "stop asking why" all the time. They had not been included in discussions about how we were going about continuous improvement and why their involvement was important. They had not been recognized as part of the problem-solving team.

3. *Responsibility is not clearly defined.* Choosing exclusively technical or operations personnel to be responsible for root-cause analysis has its limitations. Many times, technical people are not sufficiently familiar with the details of how a job is run or what happened on the last run. Many technical people tend more to want to study, collect data, and perform analysis to solve problems. Operations people, on the other hand, are not usually experienced with problem-solving tools such as experiments, statistical analysis, or basic cause-and-effect analysis. They generally have a more practical, less data-oriented viewpoint and approach. Of course, many technical people have an operating viewpoint, and vice versa. Suffice it to say, however, that a combination of skills, experiences, viewpoints, and approaches is required.

At the same investment casting company that I mentioned in the previous example, we had a case of confused responsibility that I have seen many times at other companies in my career. A process routing sequence for a part was established by the industrial engineering department. The production supervisor disagreed with various process sequences (for instance, he thought that the heat treating sequence should be performed before shot peening rather than after). So he stubbornly processed the part using his own routing sequence. Several production hourly workers who had been running the part for 25 years also thought they knew the best routing sequence and ran the part their way when they had the chance. Such chaotic parts routing is not that unusual, particularly in companies with undisciplined cultures.

4. *There may be multiple causes or a complex interaction among causes.* Some root causes can be uncovered by individuals. It may be that the root cause is relatively obvious and requires a minimal amount of inquiry. Or, while many people may have to be contacted to identify the root cause, the string of causes is not sufficiently complicated or interactive to require the involvement of more than one analyst. An example would be a late delivery that is due to

- The item being received late from the final machining department, which is due to

- Late delivery from the x-ray department, which is due to

- An excess buildup of parts ahead of the x-ray department, which is due to

- A shortage of workers because an operator was on vacation for a week, which is finally due to

- The lack of a backup plan for replacing vacation workers—the real root cause

Other, more complicated, problems require multiple skills or viewpoints in an interactive environment to identify the root cause. For example, a serious scrap and rework problem plagued a passenger car stainless steel stamped wheel cover plant. It was suspected that the problem was due to a variety of causes such as worn-out tooling, presses in need of rebuild, aggressive material handling, and recent changes to thinner gauge stainless steel. In this case, a team approach was used involving process engineers, outside equipment vendors, tool shops, hourly employees, and manufacturing supervisors. The team decided to increase the steel gauge by 3 percent and to develop a schedule of press rebuild and tool refurbishing. It took about one year to complete the changes, but scrap and rework dropped dramatically. The team approach resulted in a more realistic plan.

- Outside equipment vendors and tool shops provided a more realistic schedule for rebuild and refurbishment.
- Hourly employees provided detailed descriptions of how equipment and tooling malfunctions were causing scrap and rework.
- Manufacturing supervisors protected scheduling requirements.
- Process engineers organized and prioritized the root causes and actions needed.

When, for some nonconformance conditions, multiple skills are needed, a team comprising all of those skills is required. So what should the team look like? This obviously depends on the nature of the company and the problems involved. But for complex problems, I have found the following points useful.

1. To provide the range of skills and detailed knowledge required to find complicated root causes, a team of up to 10 persons may be required. Depending on the nature of the problem, technical, operations, supervisory, and hourly employees may need to be represented. A major difficulty is for team members to find sufficient time apart from their regular, day-to-day duties to spend on root-cause analysis. If there is a significant opportunity for manufacturing improvement, full-time team members (particularly diagnostic employees such as manufacturing engineers) should be appointed or hired. They will pay for themselves many times over. The greater and faster the improvement desired, the more dedicated time required by the diagnostic team members. Also, because complex root causes are difficult to identify, a company's most creative and experienced people should be assigned to root-cause analysis teams.

2. Proper selection of the team leader is critical. For root causes that are difficult to find, a unique combination of skills is required. The team leader must be

- Intelligent and analytical. Complex root causes require someone who thinks about cause and effect and is able to comprehend the multiple variables potentially affecting results.

- Tenacious. Patience and the ability to think through details are required to sift through the multiple levels of symptoms and causes.

- Highly motivated. This job is too difficult for a person not willing to work hard to overcome the many roadblocks to finding root causes.

- Able to work with and motivate people. This may be the most important skill of all. Eliciting relevant opinions and facts from the many people involved with manufacturing requires diplomacy, persuasion, skill in asking questions, and the ability to run a meeting effectively and efficiently.

One plant manager with whom I worked had been trying for six months to increase daily production about 15 percent in order to prepare for the new model year's increased demand. Time was running short, and we were getting desperate for results. This manager was a dictatorial person who had been ordering his staff to implement various remedies to increase production. But nothing was working. He was not a good listener; he held only one-on-one meetings with his functional heads and avoided group discussion meetings.

This plant manager was removed from his position and replaced by a manager who had less plant experience but was more participative. Incredibly, within 60 days production had increased the 15 percent we were after. He had held group discussions with his functional heads, some manufacturing supervisors, and selected hourly employees and had asked simply, "What do we have to do to quickly increase production 15 percent plus?" In one week, the group came up with a series of suggestions, including adding people to break bottlenecks and changing the methods of moving in-process parts. This resulted in the improvement.

3. Responsibility should be assigned to a team member, usually the team leader. One of the biggest reasons that root-cause analysis bogs down is vaguely defined responsibility for the root-cause task. It is a basic tenet of management that an individual, not a group, must be assigned responsibility for a task. If a group is assigned responsibility, everyone thinks the other person is responsible.

I'm not sure why this is such a difficult concept for some people to grasp. Perhaps it is ingrained in some companies' cultures. Maybe some people just want to avoid responsibility. But I have seen it played out many times.

> • When I was a new CEO, various wholesale distributor customers complained to me that our distributor programs were always late. They would receive announcements about programs after the programs started, and in some cases there was little time left to participate. These programs were put together by both the marketing and the sales departments. When I asked the heads of these departments (who were responsible for the content and timing of the programs) why the programs were late, they had no answer. Each looked at the other. No one had taken or been assigned overall responsibility. Each one completed his part of the programs, but neither was driving to meet overall deadlines. Now, however, it is clear which department head is responsible for each program and project. The result has been that we have had minimal confusion and delays and have been on time.

> • After becoming CEO of one company, I discovered that a large past-due schedule was mainly the result of production bottlenecks at three operations: x-ray testing (the quality

department), final machining (the manufacturing department), and final paperwork documentation (the engineering
department).

These departments were headed by vice presidents reporting
to the divisional general manager. None of them, nor anyone
else in the organization (for example, production scheduling),
had been assigned responsibility for breaking bottlenecks
during the day-to-day ebb and flow of operations. No one was
coordinating the solving of these bottleneck problems because
each department thought it was someone else's responsibility.
The problem was aggravated in that functions were operating
independently with minimal teamwork. Day-to-day bottlenecks were substantially alleviated by assigning overall responsibility to the manufacturing department.

4. Hourly workers should be consulted. Their involvement in
manufacturing problem solving has had many variations.

• Employee suggestion programs have been implemented
ranging from informal to very structured in which all suggestions are entered into a tracking system, every suggestion is
answered, and rewards are given. The results, however, seem to
be spotty, with some organizations reporting success and
others reporting disastrous results and program cancellations.
For example, at a division with 2000 hourly workers under
one roof, a massive quality improvement program had been
undertaken one year prior to my arrival. All employees had
been trained (classroom style) in the basics of problem solving.
As part of this training, a formal employee suggestion program
was initiated that included written employee suggestions
and rewards for those employees whose suggestions were
implemented.

Unfortunately, the quantity and quality of human resources
necessary to adequately support such a major undertaking

were lacking. Some suggestions took a year to answer, and many more than six months. When awards were distributed, the logic was weak and some people felt cheated. Jealousies arose, and workers were generally frustrated and angry. The lesson is that it is better not to start a suggestion or worker involvement program unless there are sufficient planning and resources behind it.

• Quality circles are usually defined as voluntary teams of workers organized to solve problems in their own departments and have usually not addressed multidepartmental problems. The somewhat narrow focus has produced spotty results.

• Targeted hourly employee involvement is the approach I have found most useful. The team leader, along with management members of the team, select hourly workers based on the likelihood that they will contribute to the root-cause analysis. The advantages of the targeted use of hourly employees is that unrealistic expectations (common to many broad-based involvement programs) are controlled, and that those employees most likely to contribute quality information are tapped for participation.

At the company that tried the formal employee suggestion program, the final machining operation had been a source of various problems—frequent equipment breakdowns, as well as difficulty in reaching production unit and perishable tooling unit targets. Production managers had minimal input from production workers. Then a different approach was tried. Each machine operator filled out a written problem survey about his or her machine. Workers responded with detailed lists and descriptions of a multitude of problems with the equipment. Their responses became the basis of a machine rebuild program and a preventive maintenance program, and production efficiency improved 20 percent. Supervisors were amazed by the response and continued to involve workers in solving operating problems with other items such as tooling improvement and scheduling. In this department, workers were chosen on the assumption that they would contribute in the area in which they were the experts. Some operators had been running their machinery for 20 years, but no one had ever asked them how to improve!

Another example of targeted employee involvement occurred in the mid-1970s. As many as eight hours were necessary to change part numbers on a heavy duty rear axle differential case casting. The line was highly automated, with multiple machining stations (drilling, tapping, cutting), but in the mid-1970s, quick change tooling was not generally designed into the equipment. The long changeovers were jeopardizing production as quantity requirements rose. Somewhat out of desperation, supervisors chose several machine operators, a maintenance employee, and a tool room employee and asked their opinions about how to cut setup time on this line. The employees were chosen based on their experience on this line for a targeted problem for which they would be likely to contribute to the solution.

From these discussions came various suggestions that were adopted.

—Tooling storage was reorganized to improve storage location identification and record keeping.

—Tooling was reviewed after each run to correct problems before the next run.

—Tooling was collected and stored for each machine location in the line before the line was shut down for changeovers.

—Setup time was reduced to two hours.

- Empowered employee teams are created by passing on a portion of decision-making authority and responsibility to employees. Employees experience a sense of ownership and control over their jobs, and feel more responsible. They show more initiative in their work, accomplish more, and enjoy their work more. As managers and employees gain experience working together on continuous improvement activities, the possibilities for more empowered teams increase. This concept has great potential as long as management stays involved and does not abandon responsibility for keeping the organization under control.

5. Some employees should probably not be on the root-cause analysis teams. Those without the proper motivation and knowledge probably will not contribute much and could hurt the team's efforts. But there is one type of individual who should be kept off teams altogether. That is the individual who has some authority in the organization and is resistant to change. Change is inevitable in problem solving, and people, particularly those with authority, who resist change can disrupt team efforts.

Notes

1. J. M. Juran, ed., *Juran's Quality Control Handbook*, 4th ed. (New York: McGraw-Hill), 22.33–34.

2. Peter R. Scholtes, *The Team Handbook* (Madison, Wis.: Joiner Associates, 1988), 2.18–36.

Chapter 4

Major Types of Root Causes

Over the course of my career I've found a relatively consistent set of root causes common to many manufacturing plants. I'm not suggesting that the following list is complete for any or all types of plants, only that I have observed these 16 causes over a varied range of plant locations manufacturing various types of products for various companies. For each root cause I have suggested actions that might remedy them.

1. *Inadequate process instructions.* Many times, for varied reasons, written instruction as to how to precisely process a part are unavailable, outdated, illegible, or buried in a file with a morass of other information. Obviously, without written instructions, process consistency—particularly if there is an inexperienced operator or a long interval since the job was last run—is difficult to accomplish. These instructions should include items such as routing sequences, dimensional drawings, machine instructions, setup instructions (including drawings), lubricating instructions, recommended oven temperatures—in short, any processing variable that can affect the quality of a part. These instructions should be written down for every part number so that the identical process can be followed every time a part is run. A set of process instructions should be available for every department or step in the process that can affect quality. Tables 4.1, 4.2, and 4.3 represent portions of a set of forging process

instructions. With detailed process information such as that shown, there is a much greater probability that processes will be consistent and, thus, that parts will be uniform.

These and other process instructions were developed after I found inadequate written process instructions at one company. I asked a department supervisor if there were written process instructions on all part numbers. He brought me four or five folders representing different part numbers, all about 8 to 12 inches thick. Each contained a mess of disorganized paper including part prints (some out of date), old process routings, and helpful hint notes on previous production runs (some six years old). All were very dirty. After further discussion, we determined that the parts were really processed based on the individual operator's personal notes—notes that were not documented anywhere. We embarked on a major effort to revise all process instructions, starting with the most difficult. Our goal was to run higher volume jobs. The folder for each part number was to include only key information such as routings, the part print, the tooling print, and key process instructions. These documents were to be developed with the help and agreement of the operators, the process engineers, and the manufacturing engineers. What an undertaking! When I left the company after one year, we had only about 25 percent of the part numbers complete. But on those part numbers, scrap and rework were cut in half.

2. *Employee failure to follow process instructions.* Even when written process instructions are available, many times they are not followed. Certainly adequate time should be taken by supervisors or staff to explain the whats and whys of the instructions. Sufficient time should be allowed for discussion, feedback, and questions to make sure every operator understands the procedures. If a new operator is hired, he or she should be given proper training before being allowed to participate in a job.

Another problem might occur if operators know that they should follow written instructions, but don't. This can be due to various reasons such as the operators' inability to read, a mistaken assumption that they already know how to do the job, or lack of concentration. Whatever the reasons, supervisors must create an atmosphere of motivation, training, and discipline that minimizes such lapses.

In my experience I have found so few instances of adequate written process instructions that I didn't know if employees, given the chance, would follow them. In most cases, employees weren't following written instructions because they were either inadequately explained or just plain wrong.

3. *Equipment incapability or breakdown.* To the extent that equipment is not capable of holding key dimensional or other tolerances, nonconformance quality conditions will result. Periodic capability studies should be performed to determine the extent to which various pieces of equipment are capable of holding tolerances. On equipment where control charts are kept or statistical process control

Table 4.1. Forging instructions.

Basic die:	55	Control No. CS 751
Allied part(s):	None	
Material specifications:	1055 aluminum	Metallurgical heating process A22
Stock size/condition:	9″ round, blade cut, serialized with 1/8″ chamfer	
Stock coating:	stock with cilium nitrate .006 thick and pre-form with QM 7.07	
Loading procedure:	See individual operation procedure	
Pre-heat temperature/cycle:	See individual operation procedure	
High heat temperature/cycle:	See individual operation procedure	
Post forging treatment:	Air cool individually	

Table 4.2. Forging instructions.

Special Instructions
MUST FOLLOW LUBE PROCEDURE TO FINISH FORGE   **TO PREVENT STICKING IN DIE**
1. If solvus varies by more than 20°F, must readjust die and furnace temperature accordingly.
2. Must maintain bottom radius thermocouple within tolerance prior to transferring PC to die.
3. If forging sticks in I beam preform operation, cool disk 60°F below the prime temperature and thermocycle as required with maximum temperature of the I beam prime 60°F.

Table 4.3. Forging instructions.

ENTER ALL DATA BELOW INTO COMPUTER		
Maximum forging pressure	(Pounds per square inch)	( )
Maximum restrike pressure	(Pounds per square inch)	( )
RAM dwell time	(Seconds)	( )
Maximum equalization time for alert	(Seconds)	( )
Reference height	(Inches)	( )
Die setpoint temperature	(F)	( )
	Met engineer to advise	
Desired forge temperature	(F)	( )
Outer diameter/upper tolerance	(+)	( )
Outer diameter/lower tolerance	(−)	( )
Mid-radius lower tolerance	(−)	( )
Material to be forged		( )
Furnace setpoint temperature	(Zones 1–12)	( )
High tolerance alarm for zones	(+)	( )
Low tolerance alarm for zones	(−)	( )
Delay open at zero pressure	(Seconds)	( )
Strain rate	(1/minute)	( )

methods are used (discussed in chapter 2), equipment capability is continuously monitored.

Excessive machine breakdowns can cause delivery delays, increase processing time, and even cause quality and cost problems. To assist in root-cause analysis, information is needed as to which equipment is breaking down and the frequency of breakdown. Figure 4.1 shows one type of measure that identifies the lost hours due to equipment breakdown compared to the number of hours that the equipment was scheduled for production. The data is compiled for each piece of equipment in a department, for each shift, daily. From this information, problem equipment can be identified. Remedies can range from a complete preventive maintenance program to rebuilding or replacing only selected equipment. Equipment capability and breakdown is one of the biggest causes of quality, delivery, and lead time problems, as well as excessive costs. It is probable that, in most plants, not enough resources are allocated to keep equipment in top working order. Formally scheduled, aggressive, and well-funded programs are needed for preventive maintenance, repair, and rebuilds.

At a heavy truck rear axle plant, a large multiple station transfer line for differential carrier casting machining was breaking down so often that it was available for use only about 50 percent of the time. It would have become a bottleneck if it had not been operated for all three shifts—a very expensive remedy.

At an automobile wheel cover stamping plant, expenditures on equipment maintenance and tool rebuilding were minimized over a three- to four-year period in the 1970s. I'm not sure why maintenance expenditures were neglected, but, as a group executive vice president, I had taken responsibility of the plant and inherited the results of such inattention. It was a mess! Wheel covers that needed to be reworked were stacked in large piles throughout the plant. Scrap rates were high. Productivity was poor. Delivery schedules were running an average of two to four weeks late. It took more than one year to

Department

For week ending

Equipment Unit

Date	Shift		
Monday	1st	Scheduled hours	
		Lost hours	
	2nd	Scheduled hours	
		Lost hours	
	3rd	Scheduled hours	
		Lost hours	
Tuesday	1st	Scheduled hours	
		Lost hours	
	2nd	Scheduled hours	
		Lost hours	
	3rd	Scheduled hours	
		Lost hours	
Wednesday	1st	Scheduled hours	
		Lost hours	
	2nd	Scheduled hours	
		Lost hours	
	3rd	Scheduled hours	
		Lost hours	
Thursday	1st	Scheduled hours	
		Lost hours	
	2nd	Scheduled hours	
		Lost hours	
	3rd	Scheduled hours	
		Lost hours	
Friday	1st	Scheduled hours	
		Lost hours	
	2nd	Scheduled hours	
		Lost hours	
	3rd	Scheduled hours	
		Lost hours	
Weekly totals		Scheduled hours	
		Lost hours	

Figure 4.1. Unit hours lost to equipment breakdowns.

rebuild the stamping presses and rework the tooling before we could even begin to get the plant under control. Such failure to keep equipment and tooling in top shape plays havoc with quality and costs.

Obtaining quality parts that consistently run to specification, efficiently, and with few interruptions simply cannot be accomplished without such equipment programs. Much more might be accomplished by spending the time and money on maintenance programs than by spending much larger amounts on so-called state-of-the-art equipment that may take months or years to debug. Probably the most notorious example of the latter is the billions of dollars that Roger Smith spent in the 1980s on new equipment for General Motors' plants. There was very little effect on productivity.

In addition, Harmon makes a case for decentralizing maintenance into subplants or departments within a plant, rather than having one centralized maintenance function.[1] This, along with having operators do much of their machines' preventive maintenance and repair, results in greater utilization and efficiency of human resources and better equipment condition.

4. *Tooling incapability or complexity.* Tooling here refers to the form(s) used to shape the part. It is somewhat surprising that a factor as critical to quality parts as tooling is neglected to the extent that it is in many plants. All kinds of problems result from inadequate tooling quality: undersized or oversized parts, deformed parts, misaligned parts, grooved parts, and so on. A formal tool evaluation and control program is essential. Elements of such a program might include

- Post-run tooling review: After a job runs, an evaluation of the tooling is performed by a review committee comprised of inspectors, supervisors, process engineers, hourly operators, and tooling personnel. The job is evaluated by looking at such things as the number and kind of pieces scrapped, the rework required, the number of deviation submittals to customers, and the number of parts within print tolerances. Any changes required to the tooling (for example, rebuilding, repairs, or realignment) are identified and completed before the job runs again.

• Pre-run tooling review: When a part is scheduled to run, a tooling review should be held to determine if the tooling is in adequate condition to minimize the chance of creating part problems. As part of this process, a preventive maintenance program should be developed that includes checking a prearranged list of periodic tooling maintenance items.

• Organized tooling storage: A separate area of the plant should be set aside for tooling storage. Provisions should be made for storing all of the pieces of tooling required for a single part number in one location (for example, a bin or rack) and in such a way as to minimize potential damage from handling. A filing system listing all tooling pieces for a part number, and their location, is also required.

A major objective of tooling design and manufacturing should be to reduce manufacturing complexity. Tooling design should tie into a formal program of quick changeover of part number setups. Getting the tooling and die work precise and simplified early in a new part's life prevents untold grief later on.

5. *Inefficient plant layout.* If the plant layout requires a part to travel unnecessary distances in its process around the plant, the result is excess processing time, inventory and labor costs, equipment (for example, fork trucks), and plant space. However the original layout was determined, a thorough analysis diagramming the actual path a part follows will almost always result in the potential for improvement—many times a major improvement. One successful approach is to first diagram the actual path, and then assemble a team comprising manufacturing engineers, operating supervisors, operators, and anyone else who may be able to contribute. The team brainstorms about how the path might be made more efficient and shorter. If the estimated savings are sufficient, layout changes can be made.

The most extreme example I have experienced occurred when I took responsibility as group vice president for an aluminum wheel manufacturing plant that had just been purchased by Rockwell International. Manufacturing was occurring in three separate buildings—wheel casting in one building, heat treat through rough machining in a separate building 100 yards away, and final machining and clear coat painting eight blocks away.

Both managers and hourly employees worked together to combine all operations into one building by eliminating some process steps (multiple heat treat and inspections) and by developing an efficient plant layout with a continuous process flow and minimal in-process material movement. Labor efficiency improved 30 percent. Another benefit was that we all were in one location, the original heat treat building.

At a Brazilian stamped steel wheel plant, I hired a plant manager from a Bendix plant in Brazil. He recommended a new plant layout that transformed a batch process that was spread all over the plant to a continuous flow process. The changes were completed within one year, and productivity improved by 20 percent.

6. *Inefficient process routing.* Similar to an inefficient plant layout, excessive or inappropriate routing steps can result in excess processing time, high inventory and labor costs, unnecessary equipment, excessive scrap material, and wasted plant space. Again, a thorough analysis of the need and rationale for all the routing steps for a part can lead to major improvements. One reason that too many routing steps are created is that some process engineers take an overly conservative approach to routing. Whether they may be insufficiently knowledgeable about the part and process, or whether they fear quality problems later, they overdesign the routing, just to be safe. Some typical examples are excessive inspection tests (such as sonic or magnoglow to inspect for cracks or porosity) or too many heat treat cycles to obtain the proper metallurgical characteristics. Just as it can

for inefficient plant layouts, the team approach can correct inefficient process routing. Many times, operators—particularly those who have been on their jobs for many years—know more about how a part should be processed than process engineers do.

A word of caution, however, is in order. Changing a process routing is one way to get into quality trouble. Before changes in routing are put into effect for production quantities, it is essential to run experiments to gauge the possible negative effects of process sequence changes. It is also essential to change one routing variable at a time. This avoids confusion if problems result.

I purchased an investment casting manufacturing company as a leveraged buyout in 1987. Investment casting is a process that starts by making a wax impression of a part (usually 6 to 18 inches in diameter) in a mold. The wax impression is dipped into a liquid ceramic solution that hardens when it dries around the wax impression. Between four and seven dipping and drying cycles are required. These ceramic molds are then placed in steam ovens to melt the wax. Molten metal is poured into the resulting mold to form a rough casting.

As president and owner with a big bank note to pay down, I was in a hurry to reduce costs and improve cash flow. In its attempt to reduce the very high scrap rates due to cracked molds during pouring metal into the molds our management team identified several opportunities—which we tried all at once. We made several changes to the ceramic dipping solution chemistry in order to reduce the number of dipping and drying cycles. With a goal of using less material, we changed the material and configurations of the disposable dipping sticks. (Dipping sticks are what the operators hold as they dip the wax impressions into the ceramic solution.) We altered the pouring temperature of the metal.

The scrap rate increased, deliveries became a problem, and we didn't know why. We had to go back to the original methods before we stabilized production at the prior levels. It took four months to return to the point where we started because we hadn't made provision for the old dipping stick capability. Our customers were mad, our costs went up, and we were almost pushed into bankruptcy. Boy, had I screwed up! Fortunately, we worked the problem out and got back on schedule with our customers by changing back to the original processes.

7. *Inferior quality of vendor material and/or untimely delivery.* To the extent that incoming material from vendors does not meet required specifications, quality problems can result. Late deliveries from vendors result in late deliveries and excessive lead times to customers. A formal evaluation program can be used to strongly encourage vendors to continuously improve their quality, delivery, lead time, and cost. A vendor evaluation program that we introduced at a forging company provides examples of some of the elements that such a program should contain.

• There should be a numerical evaluation of the vendor elements having the most effect on quality, delivery, lead time, and cost. Table 4.4 represents a rating system used for raw material vendors. This method rates a vendor 40 percent on metallurgical quality, 50 percent on selected physical quality items, and 10 percent on other items such as early and late shipment.

• The vendor's performance should be rated (overall and by category) for a time period relative to its competitors (see Table 4.5). The rating should be trended over time.

• A corrective action request from the customer to the vendor should be initiated every time there is a problem caused by a vendor (see Table 4.6). Information is provided to the vendor as to the nature of the problem. The vendor must identify the cause, the action being taken to remedy the cause, the dates involved, and comments. Continual discussion takes place with the vendor until the customer is satisfied that the problem is solved.

Table 4.4. Vendor evaluation—Raw material weighting factors.

Metallurgical Quality (40%)		Physical Quality (50%)		Commercial (10%)	
Points	Description	Points	Description	Points	Description
100 Max	Chemistry	40	Bar identity	Max	Early shipment
	Mechanical	20			Late shipment
	property		Bar surface	50	
	Physical				
	property				Under-shipment
	Microcleanliness/		Bar radius		
	inclusions			30	
	Macrostructure		Bar length		
	Microstructure/	20	Bar straightness		
	grain size				Over-shipment
	Ultrasonic		Bar end	20	Invoice
	Magnaglow				Acknowledgments
	Mill process		Section		
	variation		uniformity		Packing list/
	Mill process				shipping notice
	change	20	Excessive drops		
	Incomplete				Response to
	certifications				inquiries
	Incorrect				
	certifications				
	Incomplete				
	documentation				
	Incorrect				
	documentation				
	Miscellaneous		Miscellaneous		Miscellaneous

• Suggestions by the customer as to what actions the vendor should take to improve should be periodically (quarterly, in this case) provided and reviewed. Table 4.7 shows such a list. Periodic ratings and continual discussion must take place to realize vendors' continuous improvement.

Table 4.5. Performance rating (weighted average): January through September—1989.

Metal Vendor	40% Metallurgical	50% Physical	10% Commercial	Overall Rating	Total # of heats	Total # of items
A	98.4	98.1	88.1	95.3	125	26
B	96.1	100.0	99.6	97.9	77	24
C	95.9	99.2	77.9	91.2	461	37
D	90.8	100.0	81.3	89.8	69	24
E	90.5	100.0	66.2	85.1	28	16
F	96.8	100.0	98.1	97.8	69	21
G	91.7	100.0	100.0	95.9	8	10

This program was introduced about six months before I left the company, so I don't have any quantitative results. But a similar program at the investment casting manufacturing company that I headed cut late deliveries due to vendor problems in half.

In chapter 1, the importance of reaching agreement with customers (Box 2) regarding customer requirement measures was emphasized. Just as it is with customers, it is critical to agree with vendors about the measures that will be used to evaluate their performance.

Besides implementing a formal evaluation program, companies must become much more knowledgeable about and more closely associated with their suppliers. There is much talk today about companies becoming "partners" with their vendors. In too many cases, this means that the companies want lower prices and more services while giving little in return. It does not have to be this way, however. Companies should pare down the number of suppliers to those providing better quality and delivery, thereby providing these suppliers more volume. As supplier capability improves, incoming inspection can be reduced or eliminated, and there will be fewer quality problems

Table 4.6. Overview of corrective action requests: 2nd quarter and 3rd quarter 1989.

Metal Vendor	Custom Action Request #	Material	Problem	Cause	Action	Compliance Date	Customer Approval	Comments
A	5	1040 Steel	Ultrasonic indications	To be determined	Microprobe analysis (material returned) samples of "A"	10/15/89		Upon completion of sample evaluation "A" will submit findings
	6	1040 Steel	Macrostructure segregation	To be determined	Metallographic review samples at "A" (material rejected)	10/15/89		Must complete sample evaluation and submit findings
B (Ingot)	Presently no active corrective action requests							
B (Billet)	1	1020 Steel	High hydrogen	Inadequate sampling	Resample in two positions	Complete	7/26/89	
C	2	822	Microstructure grain size	Unrecrystallized	Reviewing conversion process	9/30/89		"C" will be installing 5000-ton operation 2/90. Currently reviewing conversion process to improve billet product prior to 2/90.
D	3	822	Microstructure grain size	Unrecrystallized grains	Eliminate 2nd homogenization	Complete	8/6/89	

Table 4.7. What does ABC company need to do?

A. Improve product performance
B. Improve quality system to comply with customer company purchase order requirements and material specifications
C. Work to eliminate coarse grains in billet product
D. Develop a method to improve detection of, or testing to identify, quality problems prior to shipment
Example: Etch full-length billets to detect coarse grains on outside diameter areas
E. Provide a material backup program to prevent delivery delays based on product quality problems
F. Improve response time to cause and corrective action request
G. Improve delivery performance
H. Improve cost—lower billet prices
I. Reduce throughput time
J. Continuously improve

with supplier materials throughout the manufacturing process. The benefits of such dramatically improved supplier quality, delivery, and response time are enormous.

However, getting suppliers to these levels takes time and effort. The key elements of such a program are the following.

- Reduce the number of suppliers, retaining only those most likely to perform the best. A reduced number is necessary because more time and effort will be spent with them. Their incentive is increased volume.

- Assign a full-time team to visit the chosen suppliers to help them improve quality, delivery, lead time, and costs. The same continuous improvement manufacturing management processes that should be used at your company also need to be implemented at supplier companies. If this is to be truly effective, it will take a full-time effort by more than purchasing personnel.

- Involve top management from both supplier and customer companies with each other. The magnitude of such an undertaking, of course, requires their support and leadership.

8. *Difficult or complex part design.* Whether a part is designed within the manufacturing organization or outside of it (such as the case when an industrial products company makes a part for its customer's design), there must be dialog as early as possible between the design authority and manufacturing about the manufacturability of the part. The old story about designers "throwing the design over the wall" to manufacturing with minimal or no dialog about manufacturability is true in too many cases.

One manufacturing company had several high-volume designs that would run erratically between 10 percent and 50 percent scrap. These part numbers had been running this way for three years, and no causal factors had been identified. It was impossible to know for any production run what the scrap rate was going to be. This played havoc with production schedules and caused late deliveries.

These designs contained several internal passages with tight turns, and the ceramic material forming the mold would clog these passages. In their attempts to pick the ceramic material from these passages, rework operators would crack many molds which, of course, would have to be scrapped. After many months, two customers agreed to redesign these parts and pay for the tooling, a move that reduced scrap rates significantly to better than average levels. Everyone concluded that the original design was too complex for the manufacturing process. Had this been determined earlier (preferably at the original design stage), years of excessive costs and late deliveries could have been avoided.

To minimize quality and manufacturing delays, this dialog must be formally established. Formal, written signoff approval from manufacturing should be required for all designs, and design engineering and manufacturing engineering departments should be in the same physical location. When the design is provided by a customer, allowing manufacturing engineers to visit the customer's design engineers, or even to assist for a time at the customer's location should be considered.

9. *Inadequate operator and supervisor training and instructions.* How many times do we see operators and supervisors forced to tackle jobs that they are not ready for and then hear complaints that they are not doing the job properly? Too many! Certainly everyone is busy, but the failure to take time initially to train people who are new on the job results in much more time spent on correcting problems than would be required for training in the first place.

When I was manufacturing manager at a plant in the mid-1970s, production schedules had fallen off, and we had a major employee layoff. According to our union agreement, major job bumping took place so we had to employ as many workers as possible in other jobs. The result was that some 20 percent of one department's machine operators were running equipment with which they had no experience. Box makers (packagers) ended up running lathes. To minimize production loss, operators received almost no training on the unfamiliar equipment.

I was in something of a training assignment and had little manufacturing experience; I didn't know any better, so I just went along. But with the scrap, rework, poor productivity, and late deliveries due to the inexperience of these operators, we would have been much better off to have cancelled a day of production in order to train operators and give them time to practice.

Examples of the types of training that could improve operations are

- Process instructions (item 1 in this section)
- Inspection gauge usage

- Safety
- Statistical process control
- Blueprint reading
- Basic mathematics
- Equipment use and qualifications

Additional training for supervisors might include

- Setting targets for efficient human resource management, such as estimating the amount of time various types of repairs should take, or creating production targets for various pieces of equipment
- Managing time efficiently
- Interpreting union contracts and personnel policy

Each organization needs to define the training required for its type of operation and situation as well as the training most needed to improve quality, delivery, and lead time, and to reduce cost. Then a schedule should be set up delineating who will be trained on what subjects and when. As much of the training as feasible should take place at the work stations or in manufacturing departments. For example, generic classroom training on statistical process control, inspection gage usage, or equipment use will be forgotten long before an operator has a chance to employ it. Training given at the machine while running parts is much more effective. The same is true for supervisors. Holding a classroom session on union contract interpretation will be nowhere near as effective as showing the supervisor how to handle actual grievances on the floor or in griev-ance meetings.

10. *Inadequate departmental support functions—methods and paperwork.* It is known that, in some manufacturing companies, the percentage of time devoted to actually processing the part is 25 percent or less. This includes the period from order placement to shipment,

including all documentation. One reason for this is the time support departments need to get their jobs done. An example is a company that fabricates a new part. A typical set of requirements might be

(Bill of material and routing departments)

- Sales order package (customer specifications)
- Process engineering (routing and timing)
- Metallurgical
- Sonic methods
- Quality standards
- Computer design modeling
- Nondestructive testing

(Tool and die departments)

- Die design and execution
- Die preparation and manufacturing
- Machine tool design
- Machine tool preparation and manufacturing

Thus there are 11 departments that can potentially delay delivery. If these departments are not properly managed, they will cause delays. The potential impact of these departments on manufacturing timing is shown in Figure 4.2, which depicts the functions of various support groups and when they must have their work finished to meet the promised delivery date. To meet the deadlines, the bill of materials and routing requirements must be completed prior to creating the manufacturing orders (directions to manufacturing), which must be done before manufacturing begins. To finish forge by the target date, die design engineering and die room manufacturing and preparation must also be complete. Furthermore, to finish machine by the target date, tool design engineering, tool manufacturing, numerical control tape engineering, and tool kit assembly must all be completed on

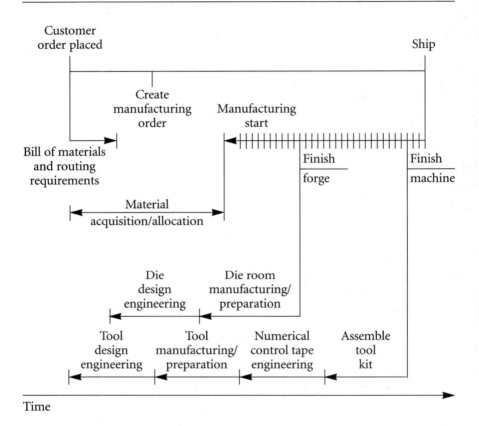

Figure 4.2. Part-time line: Support departments and functions required to prepare for manufacturing a part.

time. In order to minimize any delays caused by these departments, a system should be developed so that each department

- Sets target times for processing various types of work
- Measures actual times against target times
- Determines root causes for any time variances
- Implements remedies for these root causes
- Reviews results, causes, and remedies monthly

In one company we analyzed each support department's response time by measuring

- The *actual time* it took to process work through various departments divided by the *target time* set by department supervisors. Any ratios over 100 percent reflect longer actual times than target times. Figure 4.3 shows the results that we obtained when we analyzed the x-ray department. (The analysis was mostly a verification of the test results for each production run.) It shows that most of the jobs exceeded the target times, and seven were more than double the target time.

- The percentage of jobs completed within the time estimated by department supervisors. Figure 4.4 shows the results, again for the x-ray department. For the three months, the department met only 40 percent of the times estimated. Results were similar for almost all other support departments.

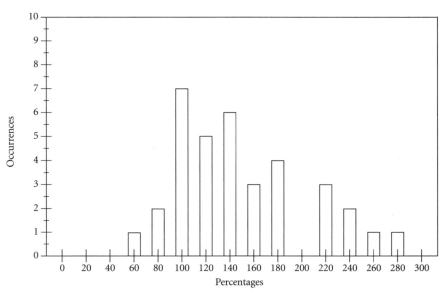

Figure 4.3. X-ray department, job performance: Percent of target time.

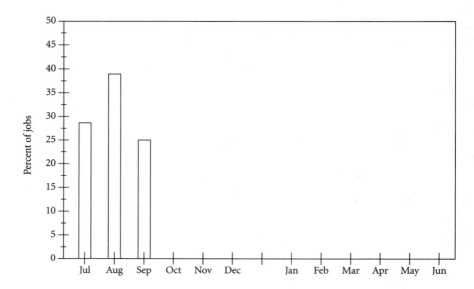

Figure 4.4. X-ray department, job performance: Jobs meeting schedule.

One month after these results were published—before much causal analysis took place, and without changing the supervisors' estimates—75 percent of the jobs were completed within target times and were meeting schedules. This was accomplished simply by calling attention to important targets, measuring against them, and then communicating results to employees.

11. *Restrictive union contract provisions.* Some examples of restrictive contract provisions are

- An excessive number of job classifications, resulting in inefficient use of workers. We've all heard of horror stories like the pipefitter, the electrician, and the laborer. The electrician has to call for the pipefitter because the electrical wire must run through a pipe. The pipefitter has to call for the laborer to carry the pipe from one side of the department to the other.

If these classifications were not jealously protected by some unions, one person could have done this job.

• Unions fighting the concept of split shifts or flexible work hours during the week. For example, if it is more efficient to run a department seven days a week (as is the case with heat treat), inflexible work hours result in a company having to pay workers premium overtime pay for Saturday and Sunday instead of allowing some workers to work 40 hours Wednesday through Sunday as straight time.

• Companies insisting on incentive pay based on the number of parts produced. This piece-rate approach can play havoc with quality.

In one company, operators were compensated according to the number of parts they produced. The union had agreed, in the incentive contract, that the number of scrap pieces would be deducted from the quantity used to calculate the incentive dollar amount. However, the contract also stipulated that the scrap had to have been produced because of operator errors. This language was not defined well, and, in practice, scrap was rarely able to be deducted. Thus the operators had little motivation to fix the root causes of scrap.

There are many, many other examples. But no matter who is responsible for the contract language, managers must take the initiative in convincing the union to allow improvements in quality, delivery, lead time, and costs. The union must be convinced that such improvements are for the health of the company and the benefit of workers. To aid in obtaining such contract language, managers must explain to union leadership and members the nature of the competition and economics in their industry, and they must be willing to compromise on other issues such as job security.

12. *Equipment or operation bottlenecks.* A bottleneck exists if, for whatever reasons, the time available to process a quantity of parts is insufficient to meet shipping deadlines. The more often bottlenecks are tolerated, the more delivery delays will result.

Thus, there must be a formal analysis that calculates the schedule requirements for every operation in the manufacturing process. There must be a proper mix of equipment, human resources, and time (the number of hours that equipment runs) to accommodate each operation. And as shipping quantities change, this matching analysis must take place again and again.

13. *Excessive setup time.* Manufacturing lead time can be reduced by reducing the time required to change tooling and equipment for different part numbers. The more changeover setups required for a given plant, the more opportunity exists to reduce production lead time. Various books on manufacturing contain excellent discussions of methods to reduce setup time.[2] Most discuss internal and external setup. Internal setup refers to those steps that require the equipment to be stopped; external setup refers to those steps that can be performed while the equipment is operating. Wontuck recommends a three-step process.

1. Eliminate external downtime. Perform the external setup while the equipment is running.

2. Study the remaining internal setup time, develop the best methods to achieve the setup, and practice the internal setup to reduce the time required.

3. Eliminate adjustments in the setup actions. Work on determining preset points ahead of time so that, if adjustments are required, they have been predetermined.

These and other actions described in these books have reduced setup times by 90 percent in many cases. Also, by precisely determining preset points ahead of time, the time-consuming and expensive trial and error method of finalizing the setup is minimized or eliminated. To determine the improvement made in setup times, the time required for major setups should be measured and a log record maintained.

14. *Excessive production batch sizes.* Again, manufacturing lead times can be reduced by minimizing the number of batch sizes that are significantly larger than what is needed for shipment. The excess quantity typically goes into inventory, resulting in longer lead times, excess inventory, and higher costs.

One manufacturing company had numerous, relatively small regional manufacturing plants set up to manufacture customer special orders. Many branch warehouses throughout the country acted as inventory warehouses for quantity orders. Since the daily special order quantities from regional plants varied dramatically, the regional plants often had to choose between sending people home early or manufacturing larger batch sizes and building inventory to keep workers busy. Over many years, they elected to run large batch sizes and build inventory; they ended up with excess inventory, a fair amount of it unusable because of the special order nature of some part numbers. Some remedies for excessive batch sizes can be found in most of the books describing just-in-time concepts.[3]

15. *Employee concern for job security.* If employees think their jobs are threatened because of continuous improvement, it is difficult to get many of them to generate much enthusiasm for participation in such activities. The more successful that continuous improvement is in improving quality, delivery, and lead times, the less the need will be for direct and indirect labor at the same level of demand. This is due to improved product flow and less scrap and rework. In fact, improved labor productivity can generate the biggest cost savings from continuous improvement.

Probably the best way to obtain savings due to increased labor productivity is to increase unit volume at a similar level of labor.

Employees see more volume with minimal layoffs. Increased unit volume can occur when the total market for a product is growing and most competitors are benefiting from this growth. When the total market is stable or shrinking, however, a company must gain market share to increase unit volume. This can eventually happen as continuous improvement reaps a competitive advantage in quality, delivery, and lead time. However, if such an advantage is gained, there will probably be a lag time between that advantage and actual market share improvements, resulting in a period of excess labor.

An excess labor situation may be alleviated by normal attrition. Normal attrition may be high either because an older workforce enters retirement age or because employees change jobs, such as exists in a highly competitive job market. A fair amount of attrition is also due to many workers voluntarily leaving after continuous improvement activities have been going on a while because they feel they don't fit in with the new environment. Some employees just can't get comfortable with an environment of continual change.

When attrition alone does not absorb excess labor, sometimes retraining and assignment to other departments is possible. Many knowledgeable plant employees, with proper training and experience, can make valuable contributions as inside or outside sales people, marketing staff, or engineering employees. Early retirement programs can also help reduce excess labor. This method was used by many companies in the restructuring layoffs that occurred in the early 1990s.

When these methods fail to reduce excess labor quickly enough, a company must decide whether to absorb excess labor costs for a longer period of time or to lay off employees. There is extreme pressure to lay off employees when the survival of a company is threatened by poor financial results or the jobs of top executives are threatened by impatient boards or owners looking for better financial results. The temptation is great to go for the short-term benefits of layoffs.

When I was in charge of manufacturing for four plants for an automotive supplier, we presented a three-year manufacturing plan to improve productivity and quality. Part of that plan was to hire several process engineers and quality personnel to accomplish these objectives. The plan was received with enthusiasm by division and automotive operations top management. But two days later, when we presented our manufacturing plan for the next year, we were told to cut head count 5 percent and freeze hiring for that year. When I asked how this plan tied in with our three-year plan of improving productivity and quality, I was told to do it without hiring the process engineers and quality personnel. I came to find out that this type of thinking was quite common in the 1980s and still exists in too many cases.

I'm sure that, in some instances, there is no other way to survive but by laying off people when continuous improvement activities result in excess labor. However, my experience tells me that layoffs should be viewed as a last resort. When I was involved in such layoffs as head of manufacturing for an automotive supplier and as CEO at a forging company, employee contribution to continuous improvement suffered greatly. If a company is able and willing to promise employees that continuous improvement efforts will not lead to layoffs, and then prove it when improvements are achieved, chances are that employees' concerns for job security will not be a cause for failing to achieve significant results in quality, delivery, lead time, and cost reduction. At an aftermarket manufacturer of radiators and heaters, we had instituted gainsharing at various plants, and as part of that program had committed not to lay off employees if improvements were made. We found that such commitments were much more important during the early phase of continuous improvement efforts than later, after employees saw the benefits of such improvements and that the company's commitment to continuous improvement was serious.

If a company's financial condition is so dire that its survival is truly at stake, going directly to employees to explain the situation and telling them that their jobs as well as the company's survival are in jeopardy is probably the best approach. Employees may work toward significant improvements even though improvements may mean layoffs. The principle of sacrificing a few for the good of the whole will be accepted in most cases, but only if employees really believe their company's survival is at stake.

16. *Inadequate employee rewards.* Asking employees to participate in a total continuous improvement process is, in most cases, asking them to put forth a serious effort to change their day-to-day behavior. They are being asked to continuously identify new opportunities for improvement in quality, delivery, lead time, and cost reduction. Their motivation to do so in some instances may be related exclusively to job security and company survival. However, it has been my experience that sharing some piece of the financial gain with employees motivates them to participate in continuous improvement activities; conversely, failing to share such gains can deter their participation. In his book on pay and organization development, Lawler states, "When the impact of a change program on the reward system is not taken into account, the reward system can become an important impediment to individuals accepting the change."[4]

A compensation program that has worked at one manufacturer ties monthly bonuses to a gainsharing formula based on cost improvements over last year's cost base. The compensation program also provides for pay increases based on job skill improvements. As employees gain job skills through training, they become more valuable to a company as they can fill in for absenteeism, vacations, and attrition rather than having extra employees around for such contingencies. As more employees gain a wider set of skills, lower labor levels are required resulting in lower costs. There are no annual general increases, only increases tied to cost and skill improvements.

Employees seem to like this control over pay increases. Plants under this formula have shown annual labor productivity improvements of 10 percent to 30 percent within two years.

As mentioned in chapter 1, these root causes of nonconformance to customer requirements act as electric current resistors in that, to the extent they are not remedied, they will reduce the effectiveness of the continuous improvement process. However, identifying root causes (Box 4) is an essential element of the continuous improvement process.

As mentioned previously, I have found these 16 root causes of nonconformance to customer requirements and financial goals to exist quite consistently throughout my career. Obviously, there are root causes not mentioned in this book diluting improvement for different companies. The challenge is for each company to identify to what extent the 16 mentioned in this book, and any additional root causes, are acting as resistors to continuous improvement at their company.

Measuring Improvement in Root Causes

In chapter 2 we discussed the importance of measuring progress in meeting the customer requirements of quality, delivery, and lead time. We said that these measurements are critical for determining to what extent the actions taken to solve the root causes of missed requirements are working. One problem in using only these measures, however, is that if they show that there has been no improvement, they do not tell us the reason for the lack of improvement. Thus, it would be wise to develop measures, wherever possible, of the extent to which root causes are being remedied.

Of the 16 generic types of root causes mentioned in this chapter, recommended measures for four of them allow trend tracking as to the degree of improvement: equipment capability and breakdowns, vendor material quality and delivery, departmental support function timeliness, and excess setup time. For the rest, programs should be developed to formally evaluate improvements (for example, plant layout and routing discussed earlier in this chapter). Also, written departmental procedures should be developed for ongoing actions (chapter 5) and periodically audited for conformance (chapter 6).

Notes

1. Roy L. Harmon, Reinventing the Factory II (New York: Free Press, 1992), 333–41.

2. Yashuhiro Monden, Toyota Production System (Norcross, Ga.: Institute of Industrial Engineers, 1983), 75–84; Kenneth A. Wantuck, *Just In Time for America* (Milwaukee, Wis.: The Forum, 1989), 189–222; William A. Sandras, Jr., *Just In Time: Making It Happen* (Essex Junction, Vt.: Oliver Wight, 1989), 105–18.

3. Wantuck, 20–27; Sandras, 7–24; M. Michael Umble and M. L. Srikanth, *Synchronous Manufacturing* (Cincinnati, Ohio: South-Western Publishing, 1990), 112–16.

4. Edward E. Lawler, *Pay and Organization Development* (Reading, Mass.: Addison-Wesley Publishing, 1981), 8.

Chapter 5

Identifying Actions Required to Remedy the Root Causes of Customer Requirement Nonconformance

**Continuous Improvement Manufacturing Management
Process to Meet Customer Requirements
(depicted as an electric circuit)**

4 Identify root causes of nonconformance to requirements

16 resistors (root causes)*

3 Measure current degree of conformance to customer requirements

10 Additional actions needed

1 Identify measurable major customer requirements

2 Reach agreement with customers on measurements

5 Identify actions to remedy nonconformance and timing. Categorize actions by responsible departments:
• Forge
• Heat treat
• Purchasing
• Maintenance
• Etc.

8 AMPLIFIER
Written departmental procedures for ongoing actions

9 Periodic audit of departmental procedures and other elements of the CIMMP process

6 AMPLIFIER
Organizational visibility given to actions and results by displaying them in departments and centralized location

7 Monthly top management reviews of actions and progress. Quarterly reviews for all employees

Ampmeter
High
Medium
Low

Degree of CIMMP effectiveness

*Note: See chapter 4 for a list of the 16 root causes.

It is axiomatic that the better the quality of root-cause analysis, the clearer it will be to the problem solvers what actions are necessary to remedy the nonconformance condition(s). Several examples of actions taken to remedy root causes were discussed in chapter 3. This chapter contains

- Some detailed examples of a variety of actions required to remedy root causes (Box 5)
- The need to assign responsibility for making the actions happen within a specified time period (Box 5)
- Assigning the actions in writing by departments responsible (Box 5)
- Displaying actions in each department (Box 6)
- Periodic management and employee reviews of progress on action plans and customer requirement results (Box 7)
- The need for written departmental procedures for actions that need to be performed on an ongoing basis (Box 8)

Developing Departmental Actions (Box 5)

Once it has been decided that an action is necessary to remedy a root cause, the series of steps necessary to accomplish the action must be determined. Table 5.1 lists the actions needed to remedy the root cause of wasted time in the machining department of a forging plant. The root cause was determined to be due to excessive searching for tooling parts needed for setup on equipment. As can be seen in this example, the actions required to remedy the situation have been identified.

One individual has been assigned primary responsibility for making sure each action is completed, and a time target has been set. Describing the actions in writing and assigning responsibility and deadlines accomplish several things.

- There is no misunderstanding as to exactly what must be done, by whom, and by when.

Table 5.1. Production machine #29 delivery action plan.

Tool Kit Program
Purpose: Time is wasted and productivity suffers when operators have to search for jaws, kickers, tips, etc., in order to perform their jobs. To improve this situation and improve our delivery performance, the following tool kit program is being put into place.
1. Establish and maintain 3 to 4 weeks of preliminary machining schedules, where work is available, for each work center.   Smith. Started 3/15/87—now ongoing.
2. Provide specific tool setup charts for each job.   Smith. Started 3/22/87—now ongoing.

3. Identify tool kit critical components required for each operation of each job using manual system temporarily until software is able to provide the data.
 	
    Smith. Started 4/1/87—now ongoing on a short-term basis.
    Smith. 2/1/88—conversion for 50% of jobs on P.M. schedule by 7/1/88 100% of jobs on schedule.

4. Evaluate if second machine will be required on any operation.   Smith. Started 7/1/87.
5. Assemble tool kit components for CNC machines and deliver to the scheduled units 24 to 48 hours prior to job run.   Smith. 4/1/88.

- Chances are minimized that individuals will forget about taking the actions.

- Prioritization of actions is enhanced and resource requirements can be evaluated because a department head can see all the actions that must take place for continuous improvement.

Table 5.2 shows another example of the actions required to improve quality in another machining department of the same plant. In this example, three large boring mills are to be rebuilt. The main steps required to accomplish these rebuilds are listed, along with responsibilities and timing.

Table 5.2. Quality action plan for Building #5.

Update Equipment to New CNC Controls

Purpose: Upgrading large turning equipment and providing additional capacity for computer numerically controlled (CNC) turning. Programs continue to increase demands for close tolerance turning equipment.

1. #175 14-ft. vertical boring mill—Update obsolete CNC controls

   A. Complete/approve appropriation request—Smith. RFA approved 7/9/87.

   B. Order controls—Smith. Ordered 7/9/87.

   C. Shutdown for removal—Smith. 9/7/87.

   D. Dismantle/remove machine (outside contractor)—Smith. 9/17/87.

   E. Rebuild and install new CNC controls—Smith. 1/28/88.

   F. Reinstall machine—Smith. Start 1/21/88. Expect completion 3/15/88.

   G. Dry run machine—Smith. 3/28/88.

   H. Machine fully operational—Smith. Fully operational as of 4/22/88.

   I. Train operators—3 by 6/1/88 and 3 by 9/1/88.

2. #176 and #177 14-ft. vertical boring mills—Update obsolete CNC controls

   A. Request appropriation request—Smith. Preliminary request submitted 9/17/87.

   B. Appropriation request approval—Smith. Approve 7/8/88.

   C. Balance of work to follow rebuild of #177.

I have found that the same person or team identifying the root cause or causes of nonconformance conditions is best able to prescribe the action or actions needed to remedy the nonconformance. Thus, the recommendations in chapter 3 about organizing for root-cause analysis also apply to identifying remedies or actions to correct root causes. The actions in Tables 5.1 and 5.2 were determined by the same team of workers and managers who identified the root causes of the nonconformance problems.

Appendix B contains more examples of written action plans (categorized by plant department) required to remedy root causes of customer requirement nonconformance. These examples illustrate the variety and types of remedies found in many plants.

Displaying Actions and Results in Departments (Box 6)

As discussed, root-cause analysis will result in the identification of many actions required to remedy root causes. In most cases, grouping these actions by the department responsible for accomplishment and execution will result in multiple actions for every department (production and support) in a plant. Displaying the actions to be taken and charting their progress in a prominent, easily accessible location will

- Inform all employees about what their department must do to improve results

- Give all employees a feeling of involvement

- Emphasize the importance of the employees' role in continuous improvement and encourage their suggestions

It is also recommended that all the actions of all departments be displayed at a central location so that employees can understand the whole effort and the place of their own department in it. This builds a spirit of teamwork throughout the plant.

At a forging company employing 2000 people, we held a weekend open house. Employees and their families were invited to tour the plant, and products were displayed along with large photographs of the final product applications—for example, the space shuttle solid rocket boosters, large Caterpillar tractors, and jet engines. To our surprise, however, the employees spent as much time showing their families the action lists posted in their departments as the forging products. They were proud to be contributing to plant improvements.

In addition to displaying actions to be taken and their progress, I have found it quite effective to display results or trends of improvement. This informs all employees about the level of improvement they are achieving. The improvement categories to display might include

- Quality improvement (for example, the percent of parts run within tolerance for all key characteristics for all part numbers)
- Delivery improvement (the percent of all parts shipped on time)
- Lead time improvement (the average number of days from order placement to actual readiness to ship for all orders)
- Internal customer requirement improvement (for example, the percent of time load cards arrived in the heat treat department from the quality metallurgical department 48 hours before forgings arrived)
- Improvement in other departmental objectives such as equipment setup time

Such feedback keeps everyone's attention focused on continuous improvement and provides a feeling of accomplishment. The CIMMP flowchart depicts the display of actions and results (Box 6) as a circuit amplifier, because I feel that while such communication is not absolutely essential to an optimally effective continuous improvement process, it is definitely an enhancement.

Management Reviews of Action Progress (Box 7)

A monthly meeting during which managers review all written departmental actions keeps them up to date on progress, allows them to apply pressure and make decisions where required, and lets the entire organization know they are interested and involved. To minimize data glut, exception reporting can emphasize changes in dates and actions (deletions and additions). Which managers attend the meeting can vary, but the top management driver of the continuous improvement process, such as the plant manager, should attend. I have tried holding these action update meetings quarterly, but have found progress to be much slower than when I have held monthly reviews. Employees seem to want or need followup monthly if they are to keep their attention and focus on the actions.

It is recommended that the review take place right in the department so that all department employees are aware of it. The head of the department, of course, should be present and should be the one to conduct the review.

Management Reviews of Customer Requirement Measurements and of Progress in Remedying Root Causes (Box 7)

In chapter 2 we discussed trend measurements of customer quality, delivery, and lead time. In chapter 3 we discussed developing selected trend measures on the extent to which root causes are being remedied. Management should hold monthly reviews evaluating trends in the measures of quality, delivery, and lead time, as well as the progress or lack of progress being made. Management should also review trends in root cause measures such as frequency of equipment breakdown, vendor ratings, departmental process time, and equipment setup time.

One of the most difficult lessons for inexperienced managers to learn is that many times the most logical actions simply do not achieve the expected results. Instead, multiple sequences of actions may be necessary before results appear. It is absolutely imperative that periodic measurements and reviews of these results be conducted so that the degree of progress in meeting customer requirements and remedying root causes can be measured. Without such reviews, problem solvers are shooting in the dark.

Employee Reviews (Box 7)

For employees to feel involved in the continuous improvement management process, periodic reviews (quarterly or semi-annually) should be held for all employees, both hourly and salaried, to review improvements and progress on various types of measures.

- Customer requirements—external and internal
- Remedying root causes (for example, equipment setup times)
- Departmental actions and dates

Employees want to know what is going on. They really do want to know how the company is doing. When we were late in giving employees an update, they objected. Some told me that their spouses were asking if something was wrong with the results.

The employee reviews were usually conducted in classroom settings with overhead slides. These reviews contributed to sustaining the employees' interest in and motivation for continuous improvement.

Written Departmental Procedures for Ongoing Actions (Box 8)

Some of the actions required to remedy the root causes of nonconformance to customer requirements should take place continually. For example, the tool kit program for CNC machine setups shown in Table 5.1 required that tool kit components be assembled and delivered to the scheduled units 24 to 48 hours before the job ran. If this action must take place every time a job runs, a mechanism is needed to ensure that the procedure does indeed take place every time. A departmental procedure manual can fulfill this need. Such a manual documents the procedures that are critical if a department is to operate consistently at an effective, efficient level.

Exhibit 5.1 is an excerpt from one company's foundry department procedures manual. The actions delineated in these procedures are specific, detailed instructions about who should be performing which

Exhibit 5.1. A hypothetical foundry department procedures manual.

Daily Production Activity

Daily activity begins with the *lineup*. The jobs to be run and operator assignments are finalized. Floor supervisors, under the direction of the general foreman are responsible for assigning tasks.

At shift startup, all foundry managers are to be out on the floor communicating with operating personnel as to quality concerns on jobs to run that day. Managers should review special techniques as identified in the foundry folder and discuss the condition of the equipment with operators. Supervisors and operators are to review *all* jobs prior to running and sign off on the job preview sheet.

The first daily scheduling meeting is held 9:30 A.M. In attendance are the foundry managers (including floor supervisors), and supervisors from production control, process control, steel stores, die room, and foundry engineering. A preliminary schedule for the next day is formulated. Information is exchanged as to readiness of stock, dies, foundry equipment, production control priorities, and human resource requirements. Also discussed at this meeting are schedules for the next week.

A final scheduling meeting is held at 10:45 A.M. with all foundry supervisors, production control schedulers, and a representative from process control. At this time, units and jobs to run the next day are finalized. Human resource requirements and starting times are established, and auxiliary equipment (i.e., furnaces and manipulators) are allocated. Information pertaining to the foundry and interdepartmental problems caused by the foundry are to be discussed at this meeting.

At 1:00 P.M. daily, the foundry general foreman, foundry engineering, and any available operators attend a die review meeting conducted by the die room. Input is given as to quality of pieces cast on dies being reviewed. The condition of dies is reviewed and disposition made.

There is a daily repair meeting at 2:00 P.M. with foundry and repair supervisors. Also invited are operators who have repair items that need attention. Unit conditions are discussed. Repairs are prioritized with input from the foundry and maintenance departments. Daily followup is given to multishift repair items. Preventive maintenance items are addressed and the coordinating of major repair projects is also reviewed at this time.

Exhibit 5.1. *(continued)*

Job Preview Meeting

1.   **Purpose**

1.1   This is the procedure to be utilized in the job preview meeting.

1.2   Meeting date: Every Thursday
      Meeting time: 1:30 P.M.
      Meeting place: Foundry conference room

1.3   Facilitator: Meeting to be chaired by the foundry department head. In his or her absence, the foundry general line supervisor, and in his or her absence, the foundry engineering supervisor will facilitate.

1.4   Participants: Representatives from foundry, foundry engineering, die room, Building #8, inspection, and west end inspection are to be present at this meeting.

2.   **Responsibilities**
      Foundry: Foundry folder
                                 Correct casting instructions
                                 Latest procedure print
                                 Latest setup print
      Foundry engineering: Process capabilities
                                 Process changes
      Inspection: Past run quality data
      Die room: Tooling status

2.1   Job previews will be conducted on all jobs listed on that week's foundry review schedule. These schedules are received in the foundry central office by 10:00 A.M. Tuesday and are distributed by early afternoon Tuesday to all departments represented at the meeting.

      Prior to the meeting, each representative is to review the foundry review schedule.

      At the meeting, all job folders will be reviewed with input from group members in their areas of responsibility. If inspection quality records show no problems, foundry folders are complete, and tooling is checked okay, the job will be declared ready for production. If there are any doubts as to tooling status or the completeness of the foundry folder, or if previous runs are incomplete or of questionable quality, the job will not be scheduled. If special instructions are required, such as lubrication technique or process changes, these will be handled via the blue sheet developed by foundry engineering.

Exhibit 5.1. *(continued)*

Jobs not cleared at their initial review meeting will be entered on the shop schedule board located in the foundry conference room and will be released when outstanding items are okayed.

Post-Run Review Meeting

1. **Purpose**
1.1 Establish a procedure to conduct a job review upon the completion of a run.

2. **Responsibilities**
2.1 Foundry engineering, foundry, and foundry clerical to follow the procedure.

3. **Definition**
3.1 Use shop floor folder as key. Post-review checkoff sheet is to be attached to the front of the folder. Foundry clerk is to use checkoff boxes upon receipt of various quality reports.

The information required to conduct a post-run review is as follows.

Department	Responsible for	Deadline (number of days after job is complete)
Foundry	End of run report	2
Building #8 inspection	Green inspection report	2
Die Room	Die review minutes	5
Foundry control	Metallurgical quality problems	2
Foundry engineering	Comments	5
Foundry operator	Comments	2
Inspection	South end inspection report	30

3.2 After a job has been run in the foundry, the main folder is returned to the clerk for filing. Contained within the main folder is the smaller shop folder. Hold tag is to be placed on the manila shop folder. As data are received, the post-review clerk is to check off the appropriate box and place the data in the manila folder. When all boxes are checked, the job is ready for post review. The main folder, including the manila folder, is to be given to the foundry engineering supervisor who will give the folder to the appropriate technician. Data will be reviewed.

Exhibit 5.1. *(continued)*

3.3   The end of run report, die review, foundry control comments, and foundry engineering comments are to be typed and placed in an appropriate area in the main folder. Inspection reports are also placed in the correct section of the folder. Operator comments are to be reviewed and, if appropriate, entered on foundry instructions, as a revision to casting instructions if the quality on the job was acceptable. The hold tag is to be removed from the shop folder.

3.4   If run quality is unacceptable, a post-review meeting with foundry and foundry engineering will be held to determine causes and corrective action.

---

actions, when the action should be performed, and who is responsible for ensuring that they are accomplished properly. The intent is to make actions consistent over time so as to minimize variations in quality and delivery. Such manuals allow everyone involved to know what key actions and procedures are to be followed to obtain maximum, consistent results.

Before this foundry department procedures manual was written, meetings took place on a hit-or-miss basis. No one knew if or when meetings would be held. They were postponed or canceled when everyday crises came up, which was much too often. Managing the foundry was best described as a fire-fighting exercise. Thirty percent of daily production schedules were being missed, and overtime was excessive. Discussions with all levels of management as well as hourly employees revealed that it was critical to have an agreed-upon, organized approach to managing the foundry. Eventually, the managers and operators agreed on a set of procedures. Three months after these procedures were implemented, only 5 percent of the production schedule was being missed, and overtime was cut in half.

Of course, there is the danger that, over time, irrelevant procedures will creep into a procedures manual. The solution to this in the case of the foundry manual was to involve employees and include only those procedures that they thought absolutely necessary.

Such procedures manuals are particularly valuable for training new personnel. In addition, when regular personnel are absent because of vacations, illness, or personal absences and replacements are necessary, procedures manuals are invaluable in training the replacements.

Again, the objective is not to have a thick departmental procedures manual stuffed full of information but to include only the information that is critical to effective, efficient, and consistent results.

In many cases, written procedures and process instructions are provided through computer systems in the plant. This makes it easier to keep the information up to date and provide it consistently to everyone. Further, some companies employ systems that walk operators through their jobs and provide online forms for capturing critical process data.

As with displaying actions and results (Box 6), I feel that written departmental procedures (Box 8) are not absolutely essential to an effective continuous improvement process. But they are definitely an enhancement. Thus, in Figure 1.2, Box 8 is shown as a circuit amplifier rather than as an essential circuit element.

Chapter 6

A Leader's Role: Auditing (Observing) Procedures and Demonstrating (Coaching) Performance Expectations (Box 9)

**Continuous Improvement Manufacturing Management
Process to Meet Customer Requirements
(depicted as an electric circuit)**

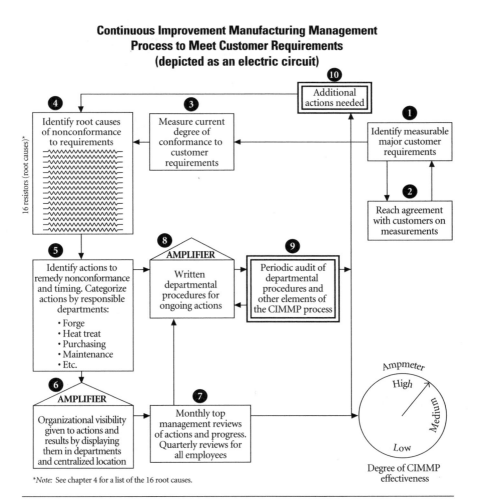

*Note: See chapter 4 for a list of the 16 root causes.

Thus far we have discussed eight elements of the recommended total continuous improvement manufacturing management process for meeting customer requirements (Boxes 1 through 8). This chapter discusses other elements critical to designing and implementing a successful continuous improvement process: auditing (observing) procedures and demonstrating (coaching) performance expectations (Box 9). The fact that additional actions to meet customer requirements (Box 10) are always needed is also discussed because we are involved in a *continuous* improvement process.

As I suggested in the Introduction, two major flaws exist in companies that fail to achieve adequate results from continuous improvement efforts.

1. Failure to combine the elements contributing to major improvement into a total process

2. Failure of leadership at the top of the organization to effectively implement such a total process

By failure of leadership, I specifically mean the failure of top managers to spend enough time *observing* employees' continuous improvement activities and *coaching* their expectations as to how to perform the various continuous improvement elements. The concepts of auditing (observing) and coaching performance expectations are somewhat related. Let's say that the forge shop department procedures manual specifies that a daily die review meeting take place to review the quality of the pieces forged on jobs completed the previous day. The condition of the dies is also reviewed relative to the quality of the forgings—the percentage of pieces scrapped, reworked, or submitted for customer deviations to print. Representatives from production supervision—including hourly employees, inspection, and the die shop are required to be present. Periodically, someone from management should also attend this meeting to make sure that all elements of the meeting procedures are being followed.

Now comes the hard part—the quality of the meeting itself. How accurate is the information on the quality of the pieces forged? How good is the judgment and logic used to determine the role of the dies in any quality problems and to determine the changes to be made to the dies? How intense is the sense of urgency to analyze and act? Who is going to answer these questions? Weak analytical ability and judgment, low performance standards, and a low sense of urgency prevent improvement in so many companies. I have observed this situation in two plants (one of which I owned). In both instances, the weaknesses were due to the fact that the people who had been responsible for performance for many years had retired. The managers who replaced them were simply not capable of accomplishing excellent performance. In both cases it took me more than six months to find this out because I was not observing problem-solving activities on the floor closely enough. Thus, valuable time that could have been used toward improvement was wasted.

This lesson—the need for personal observation and coaching of performance expectations by top executives—was a tough one for me to learn. Early in my manufacturing career, I assumed that supervisors were capable and motivated. Several other examples will demonstrate my education in realism.

As a new manufacturing manager, I spent six frustrating months trying to improve scrap rates at a heavy duty rear axle plant. Finally, I decided to spend more time on the plant floor observing what was really going on. Our manufacturing reporting sequence began with the department line supervisor, went through the general line supervisor, the machining department superintendent, the plant superintendent, and finally got to me, the manufacturing manager. I had only one year of experience in manufacturing as materials manager of two axle plants. Prior to that, I had spent 10 years in marketing at several companies, so I was quite inexperienced in manufacturing. The plant's superintendent had described to me the various procedures in effect to reduce scrap, and I had assumed they were being followed. They all sounded logical to me, and I felt confident that scrap rates would be coming down. When this didn't happen, I started asking for explanations from general line supervisors and line supervisors. Still no improvement! So I went out to observe for myself what was going on. Here's what I found.

- Daily scrap reviews were supposed to be held by the operator and the supervisor at the end of each shift to determine the causes of each piece of scrap (for example, gear forgings, or differential carrier castings). These reviews were being skipped over half the time.

- Most of these reviews, when they were held, reflected only surface analysis—"My machine malfunctioned." There was minimal probing for the nature of the malfunction, why it occurred, or the repairs that might be necessary.

- General line supervisors were supposed to analyze computer scrap reports monthly in order to identify root causes. But the reports were analyzed only when there was time, and then only in a cursory manner.

So I spent six hours a week for the next two months with all levels of manufacturing supervisors, process engineers, and equipment operators, searching for the root causes of scrap. Through this observation process, I was demonstrating my ideas of both a sense of urgency and higher standards for root-cause analysis. By the time I left this job four months later, scrap was about 10 percent lower but still had a long way to go.

After I had purchased a manufacturing company, I hired several new senior managers. I improperly assumed that day-to-day conflicts between quality problems and the shipping schedule were being resolved by the three managers. It turned out, however, that they could not get along well enough with each other to resolve these conflicts effectively and efficiently, resulting in various lingering quality problems and late deliveries. These conflicts went on for two months, and I ended up having to resolve most of them myself because of the personalities involved. Had I not become more involved in plant operations I might not have discovered the problem.

Examples of Observing the Validity of Measures

At a forging plant, the process engineering department was asked to test the life and quality of various perishable tools to see if savings could be made on such factors as initial price, number of parts run, tool life, and so on. The reported results seemed questionable, in that tooling from the vendor with the best quality reputation was reported as having the shortest life. When the test methods were examined, the process engineering department head found that variations in production, such as different part numbers being processed and different operators processing the parts, were causing variations in test results that were being attributed to differences in the tools. The tests were rerun with more tightly controlled parameters, and the results were more reliable. Had the department head not observed the process engineer's methods, the tests would have continued to be conducted improperly, and incorrect action taken.

Statistical process control classroom sessions were conducted for all hourly operators at a heavy duty truck axle plant. All operators were expected to keep their own control charts and contact their supervisors if measurements fell outside acceptable limits. The plant manager was told that SPC was being used according to headquarters' instructions. But when he went through the plant asking operators to demonstrate to him how they were plotting measures on their control charts, one-third of the operators did not know how to take the measures adequately or to plot them. Again, if the plant manager had not observed what he had been told, he probably would not have known that SPC had not been effectively implemented.

Examples of Observing the Quality of Root-Cause Analysis

An investment casting manufacturing plant had been experiencing an unexpectedly high rate of scrap because of cracked molds. Plant diagnosticians had reduced the rate of scrapped molds of a certain part number to about 20 percent, but no further progress was being made. So a retired manufacturing supervisor and a retired process engineer were temporarily brought in to help solve the problem. They determined that the humidity in the ovens used to melt the wax out of the molds was too low. Through trial and error, in one month, they reduced the molds scrapped to 5 percent. The plant employees had simply lacked the experience to diagnose the problem. It was the plant manager who determined their inexperience and, therefore, brought in the two retirees to help solve problems and train current employees.

As CEO of a company, I wanted to evaluate the adequacy of root-cause analysis. I attended a meeting in the plant of about 10 manufacturing supervisors, process engineers, and design engineers. They were trying to solve a serious productivity and scrap problem with a part. I observed that

- No hourly employees were present
- No team leader or meeting leader had been appointed
- There was a lot of bickering and finger pointing
- No dates for completion were targeted

As a result of this meeting I worked with the division general manager to develop a formal root-cause analysis approach with more employee involvement. Had I not observed for myself, how would I have determined how well root-cause analysis was being conducted?

Examples of Coaching a Sense of Urgency

As CEO of a forging company, I dropped by to sit in on a plant production meeting. A jet engine forging part that was already behind schedule had to be rescheduled from that day to later in the week. Quite a bit of time had been wasted setting up the tooling, assigning the forging team, and then setting up for another job. I asked why the job had to be rescheduled. The answer was that an engineering change to a different material that had to be prepared had failed to reach the materials department because of a communication error. A member of the production meeting put the procedural error on a list of problems to follow up with. It was a long list. I asked whose responsibility it was to ensure that the engineering change was communicated to the departments that would have to accomplish the change. The answer was that a supervisor in the engineering department was responsible. I suggested that the supervisor be called to the production meeting to explain what had happened. He arrived and explained that a glitch in a computer program had resulted in the change not getting to the materials department computer's memory. I suggested that the program be fixed and that he call my office when the repair was complete. The repair was made that very afternoon. The moral of this story is that someone needed to spend time with that group demonstrating a sense of urgency.

As CEO of another company, I attended a meeting in March whose purpose was to plan how to increase sales of a popular new product to a level that could generate more than half a million dollars of profit annually. Representatives of manufacturing, engineering, sales, and marketing were present. The needed actions were identified and assigned to various individuals. It was determined that components could be designed and manufactured and sufficient inventory could be available by September or October of that year.

But because the high-volume selling season for this part was June, July, and August, I suggested that we needed to have the part available by June. The consensus, however, seemed to be that a June date was impossible. But after brainstorming the problem, the group decided to

- Work the outside vendor tooling shop seven days a week
- Work our fabricating plant six days a week with an extra two hours of extended shifts

- Develop a PERT chart with actions and timing
- Conduct training sessions for sales representatives so that they would be ready for a June introduction

The result was that the new product was available in June in time for the selling season. And it sold well. I came away wondering who in this group was going to provide such a sense of urgency for similar programs in the future, and, after various similar experiences, we hired a new manager who brought more of a sense of urgency to the organization.

The need for auditing (observing), analytical thinking and judgment, coaching high performance expectations, and imparting a sense of urgency is required at virtually every step in the continuous improvement process.

- Are customer requirement measurements (quality, delivery, lead time) taken properly and monthly? Is the data valid or is it collected in a sloppy manner?
- Is root-cause analysis performed with sufficient depth and insight that root causes rather than symptoms are identified?
- Do the actions chosen have a high probability of remedying root causes?
- Are written departmental procedures followed consistently? Even if meetings are held, is the quality of thought sufficient to accomplish the meeting's objectives? Are performance expectations high enough?
- Are anticipated improvement results tracked against planned improvement goals?
- Do management reviews of progress reflect high performance standards and a sense of urgency to get things done correctly and on time?
- Are additional actions that are needed to meet customer requirements and improve manufacturing operations properly identified and implemented with a sense of urgency?

The better the analytical thinking and judgment, and the higher the performance expectations applied throughout the various steps in the continuous improvement process, the greater the improvement will be and the faster it will happen. So the question is who in the organization will supply the analytical thinking and judgment, high performance expectations, and sense of urgency? Top management must determine which people in the organization are able to do this. And the best way to determine this is to personally observe the people involved in such activities. In other words, detailed problem-solving activities such as root-cause analysis by teams for selected problem part numbers should be personally observed. This responsibility should not be totally delegated. To the extent that the level of performance expectations, the quality of problem-solving thought processes, and the sense of urgency must be improved, someone must continually demonstrate these through his or her direct involvement in continuous improvement activities. Improving these expectation levels and thought processes throughout the organization means spending a lot of time out in the plant observing and coaching.

Who is going to do this and how long will it take? Let's look at the parts of a somewhat typical organization, structured as shown in Figure 6.1.

Candidates For Leadership

Whoever is responsible for the results of a plant—the plant manager, division general manager, or company president—must

- Determine what the problem-solving ability is at various levels in the organization, and what the level of performance expectations and sense of urgency are, and

- Coach problem-solving methods, performance expectations, and a sense of urgency.

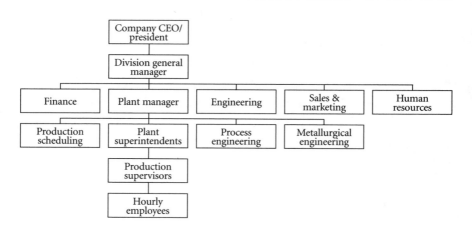

Figure 6.1. Typical organization structure.

While these responsibilities can be delegated to any line or staff managers (such as, plant manager, plant superintendent, or human resources manager), to the continuous improvement executive, to consultants, or to outside training organizations, there is no substitute for direct observation and coaching by the top line executives responsible. If they do not make their own observations, they will always have to depend on someone else's opinion about what is going on. This is probably one of the biggest failures of management in the United States. Even if they delegate this responsibility, they should observe plant operations directly often enough to be sure that they know what is going on.

Certainly such direct involvement by top managers is limited by the number of plants reporting to them, and their energy levels. But their periodic involvement on the plant floor in detailed continuous improvement activities will allow them to evaluate the success of their managers (department managers, plant managers, general managers, and so on) in implementing continuous improvement, as well as to demonstrate their expectations regarding problem-solving methods and performance standards, the level of performance, and sense of urgency. Such observation activities can certainly be limited to spot checks and can be reduced as the managers become more familiar with the employees and operations. But I cringe when I hear top management people say they don't have time for such activities.

If a major impact on results is to occur, continuous improvement activities must be aggressively implemented at all levels of a plant organization, not just by top management. Thus, in addition to the plant manager, the plant superintendent must be a strong advocate of continuous improvement activities, as must all levels of supervision, down to the first line supervisor. The best way to accomplish this is by on-the-job, on-the-floor coaching by various levels of management, starting at the top.

Many times when various levels of management get involved in such details of plant continuous improvement activities, certain serious deficiencies of the organization surface. These may include

- Inadequate root-cause diagnostic skills, due to a lack of product or process experience, or an inability to perform, or disinterest in, methodical cause-and-effect analysis.

- Inadequate people management skills. Some department managers are good technicians but not good managers of people, and they have difficulty leading and coaching continuous improvement activities.

Where these deficiencies exist, on-the-job coaching or training will not always succeed in remedying them. Some managers may have to be transferred to jobs more suited to their abilities and replaced with managers who have the necessary thinking and people skills. More diagnosticians, such as manufacturing process engineers, may have to be hired from outside the company. More talented problem solvers (for example, operators, supervision, staff) from within the company may have to be moved into key diagnostic positions or teams.

Additional Actions Required to Remedy Root Causes (Box 10)

As we have said many times, the improvement process is continuous. As the results of actions taken to remedy the root causes of nonconformance to customer requirements are measured, shortfalls will be identified. These shortfalls will become evident at various steps in the continuous improvement process, but primarily at Step 9 (auditing elements of the CIMMP process) and Step 7 (monthly top management reviews of progress). To overcome these shortfalls, additional actions (Box 10) based on additional root-cause analysis (Box 4) will be necessary.

Also, even as customer requirements and cost targets are achieved, such achievements are likely to be temporary. In this rapidly changing world, competition never rests, customers' expectations always increase, and technology keeps moving ahead.

Chapter 7

The Role of a Leader in Financial Improvement: Translating Improvement of Quality, Delivery, and Lead Time into Market Share, Profit, and Improved Cash Flow

This chapter discusses the role of a leader in financial improvement. A company that has remedied most of the root causes of nonconformance discussed in chapter 4 will have reached improved levels of quality, delivery, and lead time as compared to their competitors. Parts will process much faster through the plant. Less plant space will be needed. Equipment will be running more parts within tolerance. Tooling will be more precise both in design and manufacturing as well as capable of quick changeover setups. Scrap, rework, and submittals to customers requesting print deviations will be drastically reduced. The physical layout will be more efficient, and there will be few unnecessary processing steps. Vendors will pose fewer quality and delivery problems. Products will have been designed with manufacturability in mind. Departmental support functions will cause fewer delays. There will be fewer production bottlenecks, and batch sizes will be better matched to shipment requirements with minimal quantities going into inventory.

Such a dramatic improvement in operations can result in a substantially lower cost structure.

- Material usage can be reduced because of the lower scrap rates.

- Plant direct labor can be reduced. Because the root causes of waste, delay, and inefficiencies are alleviated, resulting in increased production speeds, there will be less unproductive direct labor time.

- Indirect labor can be reduced, because of less need for
  —Rework operations (for example, grinding or straightening).
  —Testing and retesting.
  —Inspection and reinspection.
  —Unplanned maintenance for equipment and tooling.
  —Janitors.
  —Truck drivers.
  —Support personnel (such as those needed to define requirements for routing, metallurgy, nondestructive testing, and so forth). The need for fewer support personnel would be primarily due to improved department productivity.
- Plant salary costs will be reduced because, with the direct and indirect labor reductions, there will be fewer people to supervise.
- Administrative labor will be reduced, particularly
  —Inventory control personnel because of reduced scrap, rework, past-due customer schedules, and work-in-process inventories
  —Clerical and financial personnel because fewer employees will mean less paperwork
  —Human resource personnel because there will be fewer employees

In addition, there can be major inventory reductions in

- Raw material because of supplier improvements in quality, delivery, and lead times (a result of their own continuous improvement efforts)
- Work in process because of almost all of the improvements just mentioned

• Finished goods because less finished inventory will be required for protection against internal problems that might cause missed customer schedules.

Also, once equipment and tooling is in good condition and the plant is running efficiently, less capital may be required for higher risk manufacturing investments such as highly sophisticated technology or flexible manufacturing equipment. Finally, the aggressive marketing of a company's advantages in quality, delivery, lead time, and pricing should result in increased market share.

Measuring Cost Improvement

Yes, dramatic improvements in operations can and should result in a substantially lower cost structure. But, beware! Murphy's Law applies here—If something can go wrong, it will. Also, the human desire to avoid change can surface. Managers must make it clear to the entire organization that cost reduction and profit improvement *must* be a result of continuous improvement in operations.

Just as improvements in quality, delivery, and lead time must be measured to ensure that improvement is being achieved, so must cost improvement be measured and communicated to the organization. As manufacturing operations improve, labor (direct, indirect, and salary) will be one of the largest potential reductions. Reductions in labor are potential because they will not happen automatically. Someone must identify which positions and which individuals will be eliminated. Because such actions are hard to deal with for most managers, they are difficult to achieve. A case in point: While I was plant manager of a front axle plant, our management team eliminated three positions in the forging department. I was told that the move had been implemented in June. During the monthly operations meeting in August, however, I noticed that the total direct labor dollar number for July was no lower than it had been in June. After various evasive answers, a manufacturing supervisor informed the management team that the employees had been transferred—two to the machining department and one to maintenance. This was done even though volume forecasts were down. Upon further discussion, we determined to lay off the three employees.

As we have already discussed, it may be possible to reemploy such workers elsewhere in the organization, using layoffs only as a last resort. However, in this example, we had agreed to reduce the positions. The plant superintendent had reduced the positions, but only in the forging department. No one, apparently, had told him to reduce three positions in the plant. Be careful! Even then, they might end up in another plant. The only way to know for sure is to measure.

The lesson here is to tie the specific improvement in operations (for example, less machine downtime, less rework) to specific, expected reduced costs (fewer people, less maintenance, less rework), and track those costs monthly by department and by total plant. As manufacturing operations improve, the management team should continuously review which costs can be reduced, take the actions necessary to reduce them, and measure these cost trends monthly to make sure the reductions are actually happening.

Prioritizing Continuous Improvement Projects Using Economic Benefits as the Criteria

When undertaking continuous improvement, managers should be careful not to start too many projects at once. One method of prioritizing projects is based on economic improvements such as cost savings or inventory level reductions, on which data are usually available.

The approach to prioritization should be based on the Pareto principle which generally states that the largest savings will come from a small percentage of causes, part numbers, processes, customers, and so on. Each company and plant has a different level of potential dollar improvement. Thus, before launching into improvement projects, an attempt should be made to determine the approximate potential dollar improvement and the approximate relative mix of root causes affecting a plant's performance. This can be done by examining selected data, where available, and by root-cause analysis studies using a combination of on-the-floor observations, individual employee interviews, group interviews, and brainstorming sessions.

Examining Existing Data

Examples of data that can yield information about potential cost improvements and the root causes of poor performance include

- The highest dollar value of scrap cost, rework cost, and deviations sales dollar value submitted to customers, all by part number. Examining the root causes of the scrap and rework generated by the most troublesome part numbers and finding the root causes of the highest sales dollar deviation value will make it possible to estimate potential dollar savings and inventory reduction.

- The largest dollar value of losses, by part number. Again, examining the root causes of part numbers with the largest dollar losses allows valuation of the highest potential savings.

- The highest dollar value of past-due customer schedules, by part number. These data allow the identification of potential inventory reductions by remedying the root causes of problems with those part numbers.

- Comparing actual lead times to cumulative equipment cycle times for part numbers with the highest dollar shipment. These data make it possible to identify the potential dollar amount of inventory reduction by correcting the root causes of excessive lead times.

- Analyzing where raw material, work in process, and finish inventory dollars and turns exist in the plant and why will help identify dollar opportunity for inventory reduction.

- Personnel analysis. This means reviewing the number of direct, indirect, salaried, and administrative employees by title, by department, and by shift. Evaluating the highest concentrations of numbers by directly observing how well their hour-to-hour activities are managed will help identify opportunities for reductions in personnel.
- Equipment capability and breakdown frequency records.
- Vendor quality, delivery, lead time, and cost comparison ratings and comparisons.
- Setup time documentation.

Preliminary Root-Cause Analysis Studies

Prioritization of projects can also be guided by preliminary root-cause analysis studies. Some examples are

- Layout studies. For large shipment dollar parts or part families, process engineers should document each step of the manufacturing process overlaid on a drawing of the plant layout. Arrows should represent the length and direction of each step. An interdepartmental, functional, and organizational level team should brainstorm on the floor to find a more efficient route for the parts or part families. Potential savings can be calculated by comparing the new layout to the old one. Both hourly employees and operating and staff employees should be part of the team.

- Process routing studies. For large shipment dollar parts or part families, process engineers should document the existing process routing steps. An interdepartmental, functional, and organizational level team should brainstorm a more efficient routing, eliminating steps that are not required. In many cases, final changes should be tested before they are approved. However, for prioritizing improvement projects, brainstorming can be quite beneficial.

• Process instruction studies. For large scrap and rework dollar parts or part families, process engineers should document existing written process instructions (as discussed in chapter 4). The same type of team mentioned in the first two examples should brainstorm new process instructions with the goal of minimizing the nonconformance problems.

• Individual employee interviews. Individual employee interviews should be conducted at various levels of the organization. These interviews should include direct and indirect hourly employees, first line supervisors, and key managers. The interview questions should cover subjects like how much improvement is possible; how soon can it happen; what are the various root causes of, and their relative impact on, nonconformance to customer requirements; what actions need to be taken. No more than 50 interviews are required.

• Employee group interviews and brainstorming sessions. Group interviews and brainstorming sessions should be conducted with selected groups of employees. Separate sessions should be held with hourly employees, first line supervisors, key department heads, and top managers. The questions should be similar to those for individual employee interviews.

Existing data and preliminary root-cause analysis studies should clarify some project priorities. A word of caution, however. Someone always wants to collect more data before starting. Resist this temptation. Get out on the floor and get started. I don't mean to imply that changes should be made without testing their effect on product quality. But plenty of progress can be made before such final testing.

Two other suggestions are relevant.

1. Try to choose some early projects that have a high probability of relatively quick success. This will develop momentum and nurture enthusiasm for continuous improvement instead of giving ammunition to the nay-sayers. Publicizing successes also generates enthusiasm among employees.

2. Don't try to start everything at once. Some proponents of total quality management believe that everything must be done correctly throughout the entire pipeline of supplier to customer. Such a lofty goal can deplete energies and discourage the organization. Start with high economic payback projects. Someday you may have it all right; but don't bet on it.

Using Consultants

Consultants can help a company implement a continuous improvement process. When starting such a process, it is beneficial to get help from someone who has done it correctly before because results are faster and the probability of success is greater. A consultant can be useful either as a top-level advisor or as a catalyst for project teams. However, consultants are like most other professionals. Some are excellent; they can help with your problems and give you good value for your money. Many others are suspect.[1]

Although some consultants can contribute substantially to a continuous improvement program, there are several cautions to keep in mind.

• Choose a consultant who insists that top management not only supports continuous improvement but gets involved and stays involved. Otherwise continuous improvement won't work for long after the consultant leaves. Here's an example.

Before I arrived as CEO of one company, it had spent more than $2 million in consulting fees to install a new MIS system. The system was still not being used one year after the consultant left because the users had not committed to its use, nor had they really figured out how to totally implement it. It was the company management's fault, of course, for not involving the users in the system design. But the consultant should have insisted on the involvement of both users and managers so as to prevent these implementation problems.

As published reports indicate, the state of Michigan is involved in a multimillion-dollar lawsuit of a major accounting firm because of problems in implementing its new statewide payroll system. The basis of the lawsuit is the firm's failure to involve users and managers in the design. The same concept of user and top management involvement applies to continuous improvement consulting.

• Be careful of consultants who charge large fees and insist on early payment. Some consultants typically perform a "no-obligations" audit of operations over several weeks in order to identify large potential savings. Then they bring in closing specialists who use high-pressure tactics to get payment schedule commitments with early payout completed about the time the company's estimated savings are scheduled to begin. Of course, estimated savings materialize many times, but I have heard too many sad tales of consultants who take the money and run without having produced any results. Several of these consultants have made presentations to me, and one even did a two-week audit. I decided not to contract with these consultants, both because of what I had heard and because I was uncomfortable making such large payments before I saw any results.

Many of these consulting companies will not accept jobs unless they can charge high fees (at least $500,000) based on a large number of billing hours. As the new owner of an investment casting manufacturing company with $12 million in annual sales I contacted three of these companies. None were interested in making a proposal; my company was too small.

As CEO of one manufacturing company with $120 million in annual sales, I thought we had a good plan for improving annual profits over a three-year period. The business had four product lines with a complex distribution system (through manufacturers' agents and direct to large retail accounts; direct to large wholesale distributors; and direct to radiator shops through many company-owned branch warehouses and independent sales agents' warehouses). We also had other relatively complex facilities—three main manufacturing plants, numerous smaller regional manufacturing plants, and three large regional warehouse distribution centers. With such complexities, I was looking for a consultant to look over our plans and provide an objective opinion as to whether we were heading in the right direction, whether we had forgotten something, and whether there might be other ideas that we had overlooked. But all three consulting companies contacted wanted to send in a large number of analysts. Their fee estimates ranged from $1 to $2.5 million, payable within the first six months. I was willing to pay $200,000 for some help and verification of our plan, but I could not interest these consultants in such an approach.

• Be skeptical of consultants with a narrow focus approach, particularly those with the latest fad fix. Some of the hot fads of the past—which some companies embraced with only spotty results—have been automation, quality circles, and Kanban scheduling. Now we have "reengineering" the organization, benchmarking, empowerment, and gain sharing. There is merit in all of these concepts, but, if the consultant is specializing in these approaches and you want a program to make major long-term or permanent improvements, you probably will be better off finding someone with a total approach.

• After hiring a consultant, top management should keep themselves informed of progress. When I have used consultants I have required both a schedule of the consultant's planned activities by week and a weekly meeting with me and key managers to update us on the activities of the prior week, any changes to the planned schedule, and specifics about the activities of the next week. Such an approach keeps everyone informed and minimizes the possibility that misunderstandings will derail the project.

Several recent articles warn of fad approaches to improvement. One, in the *Wall Street Journal*, points out that "while many of these trendy remedies may promise more motivated work forces and greater productivity, the results often fall short."[2] Another, in the *Washington Post,* quotes Brad Stratton, editor of *Quality Progress,* the monthly magazine of the American Society for Quality Control: "If you're not willing to make this part of your company for at least the next 10 years, then it's of no use to you."[3]

As CEO, I used to receive an average of two to three calls every week from consultants wanting to help improve quality or reduce manufacturing costs. I discouraged almost all of them by insisting on detailed answers to three questions before I even scheduled an appointment.

1. What specific approach do you use to improve and how does it differ from the approaches of other consultants? In other words, what differentiates you from your competitors? (In the answers, look for specifics like root-cause analysis, measurement, and so on.)

2. What specific examples do you have of savings on prior jobs? Where did they come from? How did you get them?

3. How do you get paid? Do you want the bulk of the fee up front or after savings start coming in?

Chances are that someone who can provide concrete answers to those questions is worth talking to.

After you have selected a consultant you think you want to work with, insist on references. *References are your best protection.* But don't just take the references the consultant gives you. Ask for a complete list of his or her last 10 projects, and then you choose whom to call. If the consultant resists, there usually is a reason.

As CEO of one company, I was close to contracting a consulting company whose initial references checked out well. I asked its representatives whom they had completed projects for in the last year so that I might check further references. They refused, claiming it was against company policy to give out the names of clients. They lost my project. When I checked further on this consulting company, I found it had a reputation for botching projects.

Notes

1. John A. Byrne, "Managing For Quality: Consultants—High Priests and Hucksters," *Business Week* Special Edition (October 25, 1991): 52–54.

2. Fred R. Bleakley, "The Best Laid Plans: Many Companies Try Management Fads Only to See Them Flop," *Wall Street Journal,* July 6, 1993, A1 and A6.

3. Jay Mathews, "Totaled Quality Management," *Washington Post,* June 6, 1993, H1 and H16.

Chapter 8

The Formality of the Continuous Improvement Process, and Other Final Observations

The Compatibility of Formality and Employee Empowerment

The continuous improvement process described in this book is relatively formal and structured. It includes

- Measuring progress in meeting customer requirements (including internal customers) and remedying root causes

- Grouping written actions by department, identifying responsibility and timing, and displaying these actions in departments

- Creating written departmental procedures manuals

- Meeting with managers and employees to review progress in satisfying customer requirements, remedying root causes, and executing actions

Even so, these relatively formal elements of communication and control are compatible with employee empowerment. Employees are still encouraged to identify improvement opportunities through root-cause analysis and the identification of needed actions. Varying degrees of freedom in doing so are still possible (including minimal management involvement), depending on the company culture. Measuring and reviewing progress by themselves do not negate empowerment. Empowerment does not mean suspending measurement and communication to management, although some proponents of empowerment would like us to believe it does.

Obviously, the degree of empowerment depends on the manner and attitudes exhibited by managers as they participate in measurement and review. If their attitudes are supportive, encouraging, tolerant, and understanding, not only can empowerment work, it will be enhanced.

This degree of formalization and structure for continuous improvement will probably not be necessary for businesses

- That are small enough to manage informally

- Whose cultures are sufficiently oriented toward problem solving and which possess good organization, discipline, a sense of urgency, and employee communication and cross-functional team involvement

- Whose customers do not require formal feedback in improvement

These businesses can adopt the elements of the continuous improvement process described here that best fit their own circumstances. However, my experience has been that plants and companies more often err on the side of too little rather than too much formalization of continuous improvement.

The Compatability of Top Management Auditing (Observing) and Employee Empowerment

One school of thought encourages top management to set goals for employees, then let the employees figure out for themselves what improvement actions should be taken. Minimum involvement by management is suggested. Periodic auditing (observing) by top management would be discouraged.

I disagree with this school of thought in that I believe the best results can be achieved if top management understands what employees are doing, so that employees and management can work together for improvement. Too many times, managers have no clue about what is going on and must rely totally on employees telling them what is happening. This is equivalent to a football coach staying in the locker room during a game and relying on the players to tell him or her what happened. That's why football coaches watch on the sidelines and review game films. They need to know exactly what happened and why, so they and the players can try to improve as a team.

Factors Contributing to the Failure to Apply a Total Continuous Improvement Process

In an attempt to understand why many companies do not use or are not attempting to develop a total continuous improvement process in manufacturing, I talked to seven quality and cost consultants about their experiences. They were ODI, Burlington, Massachusetts; Coopers & Lybrand, Detroit, Michigan; Rath and Strong, Lexington, Massachusetts; Proudfoot Corporation, Winter Park, Florida; Philip Crosby Associates, Winter Park, Florida; the Juran Institute, Wilton, Connecticut; and Gemini Consulting, Morristown, New Jersey. Some of the reasons consistently mentioned by these consultants were as follows:

• Some top managers just don't know how to go about a total process of continuous improvement, which many times results in a "quick fix" mentality. Lack of training and experience in manufacturing and in formal problem-solving techniques are two reasons. In my early manufacturing positions, I certainly did not know how to implement such a total system of continuous improvement with basic elements of planning and control. I cannot recall that any companies or plants I was aware of used such a complete process, although many individual elements of the process were being used. How was a manager to learn such a total process approach when it was seldom used in the 1970s and 1980s? Either by being exposed to one of the few companies or consultants employing total continuous improvement process methods or by trial-and-error approaches. Many times this lack of manufacturing experience leads executives to seek a quick fix to quality and cost problems. But the search for a quick fix leads away from continuous improvement methods.

• Some managers see no need for massive change. Many companies have become too comfortable. The consultants that I talked with found that some major event was typically required to jolt managers into action. One said that, in some cases, the attitude seemed to be, "If it isn't broken, don't fix it."

Some companies may have had the luxury of growth in the past. One typical reason that a company is jolted into action is getting into market share or financial trouble with banks, boards, customers, or competitors. The recent trend to board activism, which has resulted in the firings of major company CEOs, may pressure more companies to change. The globalization of markets will also create more pressure for change.

• Some companies lack a formal planning and strategic approach to running a business, instead reacting more to crises. Some managers don't like a structured, continual approach to solving problems. They would rather solve problems in a more casual way. Having worked in many U.S. plants with a variety of employees and environments (rural, city; blue collar, white collar; union, nonunion; large plants, small plants), I have found that many employees have a definite aversion to structure and formality. They don't like written lists of actions to be taken, responsibilities identified and dates of completion set, written departmental procedures.

The more casual approach works in some cases, especially when the plant is smaller and more controllable, when employees are highly motivated and technology is less complicated. But, more often, companies could benefit from a formal approach to running their businesses. Such an approach might result in the setting of goals, in earlier warnings of problems, in more awareness of competitors. And it might encourage a more formal problem-solving process.

Applying the Continuous Improvement Process to Nonmanufacturing Departments

Because the continuous improvement process recommended in this book uses elements of basic management such as planning and control, it is applicable to functional departments other than manufacturing. Any department that sets objectives (Box 1) can experience variances to these objectives (Box 3). The root causes of those variances must be found (Box 4), and the actions required to remedy the variances must be identified (Box 5). The extent to which other elements of the processes are used—for example, management reviews of action progress (Box 7) and meeting objectives progress (Box 3), written departmental procedures (Box 8), and auditing procedures (Box 9)—would depend on the types of goals being set by various departments and the nature of their operations.

Let's use an example from a sales department. This department set a goal whereby unit sales for 1993 would equal those for 1992 (Box 1). Table 8.1 shows the variances in units from 1992 to 1993 by customer (Box 3) and preliminary root causes (Box 4), as determined by the territory manager. All the difficulties of finding the "real" root causes apply for these sales variances, just as they do for manufacturing root causes.

Let's say that the customer tells the salesperson that the reason his purchase was smaller than last year's is that business is slow. The salesperson points out that other customers are either ahead of or equal to last year's orders. He asks if he can help evaluate why his customer's sales may be slow. Finally, the customer admits that he has been buying more from a competitor company because of quality problems with the salesperson's product. The salesperson points out that while there have been quality problems in the past, they have improved a great deal over the last year. The customer admits he hasn't had any real problems lately, but then asserts that the difference in price between the products is too great. The salesperson reminds

Table 8.1. Radiators, direct marketing only: June 1993 vs. June 1992.

Region	State	Trading area	Name of customer	City	'92	'93	Unit sales difference	Root cause for sales decrease
South-	TX	Lubbock	A	Andrews	60	22	−38	Price/Smith Co.
west	TX		B	Lamesa	23	1	−22	Price/Jones Co.
	TX		C	Lubbock	21	8	−13	Price/Smith Co.
	TX		D	Seminole	31	13	−18	Quality issue
	TX		E	Midland	17	1	−16	Industry slowdown
	TX		F	Odessa	13	8	−5	Price/Smith Co.
	TX		G	Lubbock	12	0	−12	Credit problem
	TX		H	Lubbock	41	30	−11	Seasonal business
	TX		I	Andrews	16	6	−10	New ownership
			Total:		234	89	−145	
	TX	Waco	J	Temple	38	8	−30	Credit hold
	TX		K	Temple	55	29	−26	Price/Jones Co.
	TX		L	Temple	11	1	−10	Price/Jones Co.
			Total:		104	38	−66	
	TX	Houston	M	Galveston	94	77	−17	Slow month
	TX		N	Galveston	14	8	−6	Credit problem
	TX		O	Galveston	48	38	−10	Slow month
			Total:		156	123	−33	
	NM	Roswell	P	Roswell	180	135	−45	New ownership
	NM		Q	Roswell	66	25	−41	Price/Jones Co.
	NM		R	Roswell	38	2	−36	Price/Jones Co.
	NM		S	Artesia	57	36	−21	Slow month
			Total:		341	198	−143	
	NM	Gallup	T	Gallup	47	8	−39	Out of business
	NM		U	Gallup	40	0	−40	Lost to Edwards

the customer about the advantages his product has over the competitor's. The customer admits that the product is worth the extra cost.

Finally, the customer reveals the real root cause for his preference for the competitor's product: the company's credit office was requiring cash in advance because two checks had bounced in one week.

When the salesperson checked with the credit office, he found that there had been a misunderstanding. The cash-in-advance order was canceled, and the customer began buying again.

This example demonstrates the complexities of root-cause analysis in an area other than manufacturing and the importance of developing close relationships between salespeople and their customers if they are to be able to identify actual root causes. Table 8.2 shows a partial list of actions (Box 5) required to remedy the unit sales variances.

A sales manager should travel with the sales representatives to determine how well they are selling suggested product features, answering objections, determining root causes, and so on. This is basically an observing (Box 9) and coaching function.

Reengineering and the Continuous Improvement Manufacturing Management Process

Reengineering is the current hot concept in management. Hammer and Champy define reengineering as "the fundamental rethinking and radical redesign of business processes to achieve dramatic improvements in critical, contemporary measures of performance, such as

Table 8.2. Radiators, direct market only: Actions to be taken to achieve unit sales targets.

- Identify all radiator and core sellers in each geographic trading area
- Develop a marketing plan with sales agencies
- Prioritize sales calls based on their market potential
- Utilize plant managers for heavy duty radiator sales calls
- Make branch managers responsible for sales calls in their delivery areas
- Make territory managers responsible for calling on radiator shops
- Institute call reports—weekly reports for branch, territory, and regional managers and agencies; monthly reports for plant managers

cost, quality, service, and speed."[1] Using this definition, the concept of reengineering fits neatly within the CIMMP process. The "redesign of business processes" correlates with "identifying actions to remedy nonconformance" (Box 5) in the CIMMP process. Their "critical measures of performance" are "measurable major customer requirements" (Box 1) in the CIMMP process.

Hammer and Champy go on to say that "reengineering seeks breakthroughs, not by enhancing existing processes, but by discarding them and replacing them with entirely new ones."[2] In the CIMMP process, it does not matter whether actions to remedy nonconformance (Box 5) are existing actions or new ones. Within the CIMMP framework, steady, incremental improvements to existing processes, as well as entirely new processes, can be evaluated. In fact, one wonders why the concept of reengineering is considered new. It could be viewed as just another way of saying that, to achieve aggressive targets regarding customer requirements and cost reduction (Box 1), more dramatic actions (Box 5) are required.

Summary
In the Introduction, I stated that two major flaws exist in companies that are unable to achieve adequate results from continuous improvement efforts. They are

1. The failure to include all of the major elements of improvement into a total process, and

2. The failure of top management to effectively lead and implement such a total process.

I have attempted to describe the necessary causal elements, represented by Boxes 1–5, 7, 9, and 10. Boxes 6 and 8 (written departmental procedures and displaying actions and results), while not necessary for optimal effectiveness, act as enhancements to the effectiveness of the continuous improvement process. The necessary eight major causal elements of the continuous improvement process can be thought of as an electric circuit with all eight elements necessary for an electric current output. For example, if all elements of the CIMMP process are effectively in place except for measuring the current degree of conformance to customer requirements (Box 3), results can be disappointing because management will not really know to what extent customer requirements are being met. Boxes 6 and 8 act as current amplifiers.

As part of Box 4 (identify root causes of nonconformance to customer requirements), 16 root causes were identified as obstacles to achieving optimal continuous improvement results. These 16 root causes can be thought of as electric current resistors in that each will reduce the process effectiveness until each is remedied. For example, if all root causes are effectively remedied, except for frequent equipment breakdowns or employee concerns for job security, results can be disappointing.

Three words are very important in the title of this book: *actual experiences* and *succeed.* I arrived at the 10 elements of the CIMMP process and the 16 root causes of nonconformance after years of experimentation and its accompanying frustrations and disappointments. However, as a result of this experimentation, I have constructed a model that has worked very well for me. I have presented actual experiences and examples of some of these experiences in arriving at this model. I believe that, if you follow this model, you, too, can make continuous improvement in manufacturing succeed for your company.

However, we made the point that unless top management offers strong leadership, the chances of success are dramatically reduced. Top managers *must* observe and demonstrate their expectations, as well as make sure that improvements in customer requirements result in financial improvements by prioritizing actions and measuring and tying financial results to improvements in customer requirements.

Finally, I have a suggestion for new and aspiring managers. Early in your career, obtain line experience where you are responsible for measured results. Most intelligent ambitious people think they know how to obtain results. But the real-world feedback you can get by measuring results (costs, sales, profits, productivity) will teach you just how difficult it is to improve, how deeply you have to think, and how persistent you have to be. No one can learn this by reading or being told by others. It must be experienced.

The continuous improvement process described in this book can achieve significant improvement in manufacturing. It requires day-to-day leadership by top management, including close observation of continuous improvement activities and results as well as demonstration and coaching about what is expected from employees. I have provided examples of the successes and failures of my more than 20 years in manufacturing in an effort to make the book a practical guide for continually improving manufacturing operations results in market share, profit, and cash flow.

Notes

1. Michael Hammer and James Champy, *Reengineering the Corporation* (New York: HarperCollins, 1993), 32.

2. Ibid., 49.

Appendix A
Selected Major Manufacturing Improvement Concepts

The purpose of this appendix is to provide readers who have had limited exposure to literature on quality management a feel for some of the basic concepts and viewpoints presented in the literature. It is not meant to be a complete summary of quality concepts or to represent all viewpoints in the literature.

Some of the major manufacturing improvement concepts that developed and are described in literature today are *just-in-time, synchronous manufacturing,* and *subplant organizations.*

Just-In-Time

Various authors define *just-in-time* somewhat differently. Kenneth A. Wantuck states that the just-in-time strategy is comprised of seven key principles.[1]

1. *Produce to exact customer demand.* This concept states that the plant will be organized to emphasize flexibility, short runs, and minimum notice time from customers. The plant will produce the exact quantity ordered by the customer instead of running larger quantities to maximize labor efficiency.

2. *Eliminate waste.* Waste is defined as anything more than the minimum amount of plant, equipment, materials, and workers

required to produce to exact customer demand. The causes of waste are

- Production problems
- Excess equipment capacity
- Insufficient preventive maintenance
- Defects and rework
- Overproduction

3. *Produce one at a time.* This concept assumes that inventory has minimal value and, in fact, creates problems by clogging up the flow of production. It states that if a plant is set up to produce one unit at a time, inventory will be restricted to only those parts produced to exact demand quantities. This strategy advocates reducing inventory, thus exposing problems, so the entire process can gradually be improved until it is almost perfect.

4. *Work for continuous improvement.* This means that plant operations should continue to improve until perfection is reached. The process, of course, is never ending because perfection will never be reached in a plant environment.

5. *Respect people.* Blue-collar workers are the most valuable people source of ideas for improvement. There are more of these workers than any other, and they spend more of their time in the plant. To tap this potential, however, they must be given the respect, stable environment, and motivation to contribute their ideas.

6. *Allow no contingencies.* This calls for a production organization that is operating so efficiently that there is no margin for error. This does create some organizational stress but this principle recommends that we "draw out our capabilities to the very limit by placing all people, equipment, and material in a state of uniform stress."[2]

7. *Emphasize the long term.* Implementing the six previous principles obviously will take much effort and time. Since such stringent goals cannot be accomplished easily, a long-term commitment is required.

William A. Sandras's concept of just-in-time emphasizes high-velocity manufacturing, moving material through a plant more quickly. To continually increase the velocity of material movement, impediments to velocity improvement must be uncovered, and their locations and causes determined and removed. The ultimate goal is zero waste due to

- Overproduction
- Waiting
- Transportation
- Stocks
- Excess motion
- Defects
- Processing itself (when necessary)[3]

Sandras's basic philosophy is that just-in-time is an ongoing process. Figure A.1 depicts his concept of manufacturing "one less at a time" to achieve zero waste. The process is basically one of identifying constraints to continuous improvement and eliminating those constraints.

Synchronous Manufacturing

Umble and Srikanth define synchronous manufacturing as a process in which parts have relatively short manufacturing lead times and materials spend very little time waiting in queues. The flow of materials through the plant is carefully synchronized, with materials moving smoothly and continuously from one operation to the next. This results in low work-in-process inventories and short manufacturing

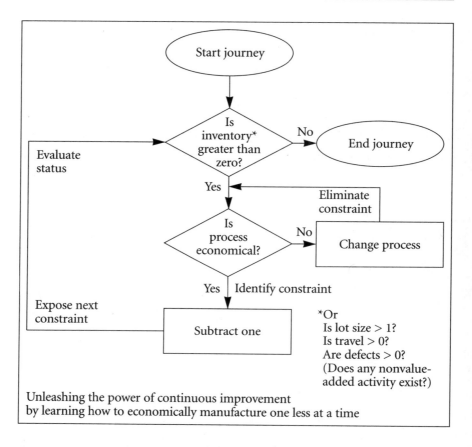

Reprinted with permission from Oliver Wight Publications.

Figure A.1. Just-in-time.

lead times. Comparing the flow of materials in a plant to the flow of a river is useful for describing both synchronous manufacturing and just-in-time concepts. Figure A.2 depicts how lower inventories allow problems to be uncovered and solutions to be actively pursued: "In the exhibit the boat has foundered upon a huge boulder. Reducing the inventory has succeeded in identifying a problem; but that problem

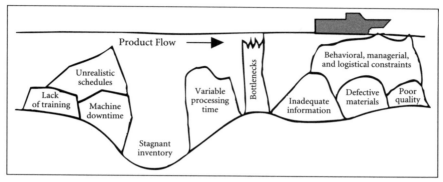

Note: Reproduced from Michael M. Umble and M. L. Srikanth, *Synchronous Manufacturing*, p. 112, with the permission of South Western College Publishing. Copyright 1990 by South Western College Publishing. All rights reserved.

Figure A.2. The just-in-time approach uncovers problems.

has temporarily scuttled the production process."[4] Also, in the concept of synchronous manufacturing, various actions must be evaluated for their effect on total plant operations rather than for selected results or departments.

Subplant or Focused Factory Organization

Harmon and Peterson state that "the reorganization of existing plants into multiple, smaller 'factories within a factory' is the single most important feature of productivity improvement."[5] Such subplants must include such functions as materials management, engineering, and maintenance to avoid bureaucratic roadblocks and delays. Harmon and Peterson suggest that the most effective subplants would be organized by product groups. Figure A.3 depicts this method.

They identify the advantages of breaking a plant into subplants as follows:

- Communications are superb because the manufacturing unit is small and people can talk to one another with ease.

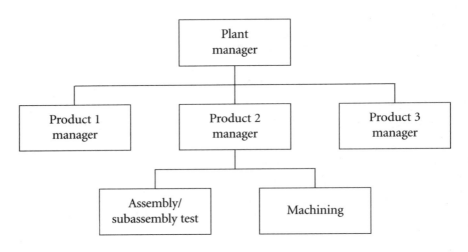

Figure A.3. Focused product organization.

- Manufacturing executives and managers control the factory on the factory floor.
- A lean administrative staff is located in the main plant, close to its employees, rather than at a separate, remote headquarters serving multiple plant locations.
- Executives, managers, and supervisors wear many hats when a business is too small to warrant hiring specialists.
- Factory support services are often provided by machine operators and assemblers. Repairs, preventive maintenance, and housekeeping are part of their responsibilities.
- Office staff is minimal and intimately familiar with factory operations, production, and inventory status.
- Everyone in the organization feels directly involved in all aspects of procurement and production.
- Limited funds and financing are available for a small factory. As a result, every individual is responsible for economizing.

The Need for a Total Manufacturing Problem-Solving Process

As useful as the previously discussed current manufacturing concepts are, as well as others such as *reengineering* and *benchmarking*, they are narrow of view in that they do not describe a total manufacturing problem-solving process. Several authors do attempt to describe an overall quality problem-solving process. Sandras, for example, uses the term *total quality control* (TQC).[6] Figure A.4 represents the process he advocates. He mentions that this is sometimes called the Deming circle or the Shewhart circle. The process begins with the *plan* section and contains such steps as the following:

- Describe the problem
- Identify someone responsible for following the problem through to a satisfying conclusion
- Explain the symptoms
- Determine the priority of the problem
- Quantify the magnitude of the problem in terms of key performance measures
- State the intermediate and long-term goals

The second section, the *do* section, requires the problem solver to describe the current situation in terms of its root cause or causes, as opposed to symptoms.

The third section is a *check* to see if the action(s) taken were effective. And, finally, the *action* section develops a countermeasure to the root cause and implements that proposed solution to the problem. If the problem was properly evaluated and the right actions taken, the measures in the *plan* section should reflect improvement. If not, then one should go back to the *do* section to do more root-cause analysis. Figure A.5 is a pictorial representation of the TQC process. Sandras states that such a flowchart "allows us to see the actual and ideal progressions of thought patterns for any product or service in a manner that will make inconsistencies more obvious."[7]

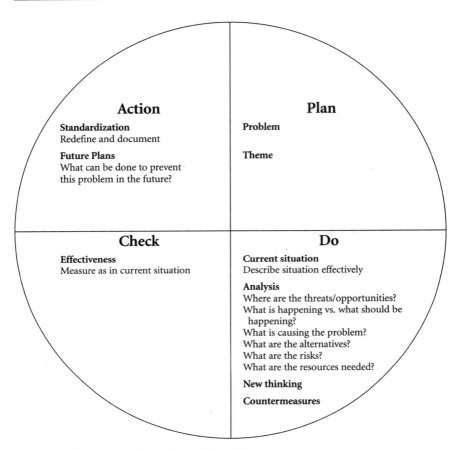

Figure A.4. The TQC process.

Umble and Srikanth recommend that after constraints to quality improvement have been identified, the following five somewhat general steps should be used to improve performance.

1. Identify the constraints in the system.

2. Determine how to exploit the constraints to improve the performance of the system.

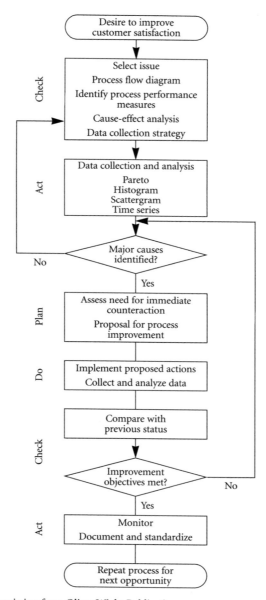

Reprinted with permission from Oliver Wight Publications.

Figure A.5. TQC process improvement flowchart.

3. Subordinate all parts of the manufacturing system to the support of Step 2.

4. Carry out the steps necessary to improve the performance of the system.

5. If, in the previous step, a constraint has been broken or a new constraint develops, go back to Step 1.[8]

In his book, *Quality is Free,* the closest Crosby gets to recommending a total manufacturing problem-solving process is his 14 steps to quality improvement.[9]

1. Management commitment

2. Quality improvement team

3. Quality measurement

4. Cost of quality evaluation

5. Quality awareness among employees

6. Corrective action

7. Establish an ad hoc committee for the zero defects program

8. Supervisor training

9. Have a zero defects day

10. Goal setting

11. Error cause removal

12. Recognition

13. Quality councils

14. Do it over again

Tompkins, in his *Winning Manufacturing,* recommends the steps in Figure A.6. He states that manufacturing is a continuous process of "improve, improve, improve."[10]

The list of additional readings provides a more extensive selection of viewpoints on quality improvement and management.

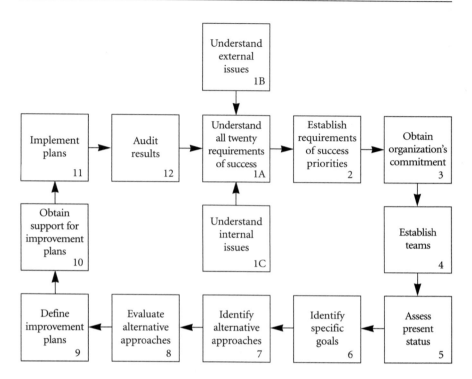

Reprinted with permission of McGraw-Hill, from J. Tompkins, *Winning Manufacturing* (New York: McGraw-Hill, 1990), 8–9.

Figure A.6. The winning manufacturing process.

Notes

1. Kenneth A. Wantuck, *Just In Time for America* (Milwaukee, Wis.: The Forum, 1989), 19–33.

2. Ibid., 32.

3. William A. Sandras, Jr., *Just In Time: Making It Happen* (Essex Junction, Vt.: Oliver Wight, 1989), 9–24.

4. Umble and Srikanth, 109–12.

5. Roy L. Harmon and Leroy D. Peterson, *Reinventing the Factory* (New York: Free Press, 1990), 12–17.

6. Sandras, 234–40.

7. Ibid., 241–42.

8. Umble and Srikanth, 95.

9. Philip B. Crosby, *Quality is Free* (New York: McGraw-Hill, 1979), 132–39.

10. James A. Tompkins, *Winning Manufacturing* (New York: McGraw-Hill, 1990), 8–9.

Appendix B

Examples of Written Action Plans Required to Remedy the Root Causes of Customer Requirement Nonconformance: Actions, Persons Responsible, Time Targets

The purpose of this appendix is to provide a variety of concrete examples of actions to remedy nonconformance (Box 5 in the CIMMP process). As recommended in chapter 5, actions should be documented in writing by department and responsibility and timing assigned. Tables 5.1 and 5.2 provide two examples of such actions and reflect that many times there are subactions required with their own responsibilities and timing. As summarized in Table B.1, these examples of actions include a variety of departments and types of actions (for example, equipment and tooling improvements, management controls, and work method organization).

Table B.1. Examples of actions to remedy customer nonconformance conditions.

Department	General Action Description
Dimensional Inspection	Restructure the gauge crib
Metallurgical Operations	Update creep/stress rupture test facility
	Establish causes of and corrective actions for identity errors in production machine area
Process Engineering	Improve engineering change controls
Quality and Technology	Identify/qualify components that can be heat treated in Building #5
Die Room	Expand tool review program
	Upgrade and improve die manufacturing equipment
Heat Treat	Heat treat tooling control
Building #5	Improve condition and reliability of equipment
	Update equipment to new CNC controls
Production Machine	Consolidate jaws and kickers into crib
Steel Stores	Upgrade radius grind units

DIMENSIONAL INSPECTION
Restructure the Gauge Crib

Purpose: Improve productivity and develop inventory
A. Plate gauges
B. Templates
C. Machine setup gages held for future requirements

1. Write an action plan. Smith, 1/2/88.

2. Establish a working catalog of current, inactive, and obsolete parts. Smith, 1/28/88.

3. Investigate storage system options. Smith, 2/28/88.

4. Develop rack and bin identification system for both internal and external storage. Smith, 5/1/88.

5. Computerize gauge crib inventory. Smith, 9/1/88.

6. Perform computer inventory of all gauges and templates. Smith, 10/1/88.

7. Dispose of all templates and gauges identified as obsolete. Catalog and store off-site all gauges and templates in the inactive category. Smith, 1/1/89.

METALLURGICAL OPERATIONS
Update Creep/Stress Rupture Test Facility

Purpose: The age of the present system results in frequent maintenance problems and the continual risk of losing creep/rupture tests. The resultant losses affect customer schedules and increase internal costs. The new system will minimize shutdown risk, reduce maintenance intervals, and improve productivity through automatic data reporting. This system will provide a state-of-the-art creep/stress rupture test system.

1. Hardware acquisition—computer, modular data acquisition system, etc. Smith, complete 7/87.

2. Finalize system software design. Smith, 2/15/88.

3. Approve software design and complete development of software program. Smith, 5/88.

4. Test system at vendor site prior to implementation. Smith, start 3/88; complete 6/7/88.

5. Begin modification of test stands and furnace upgrade. Smith, start 6/87; complete 8/88.

6. Perform initial test of system under actual operating conditions. Smith, 7/88.

7. Complete phasing in of all test stands and operating hardware for production use. Smith, 9/88.

8. Formally accept system as meeting all purchase order requirements. Smith/Jones/Edwards, 10/88.

METALLURGICAL OPERATIONS
Establish Causes of and Corrective Actions for
Identity Errors in Production Machine Area

Purpose: Wasted time, missed shipments, scrapped forgings, and customer dissatisfaction have resulted from identity errors that have occurred during reidentification of parts and test material following machining operations. A joint effort of metallurgical operations and production machine personnel will identify types of errors, their causes, and possible corrective actions which could eliminate or significantly reduce identity errors.

1. Identify error types and causes using test, inspection, and production machine personnel. Smith, 3/1/88.

2. Measure identity error problems. Smith, ongoing.

3. Review error types/causes with production machine supervisors/machine operators. Smith, 3/15/88.

4. Use brainstorming techniques to identify potential modifications/corrective actions for identity control practices now in place. Smith, 4/15/88.

5. Develop identification system and controls to be utilized in Bldg. #6 machine operation. Smith, 4/15/88.

6. Familiarize and train machine operators in new identification methods and controls. Smith, 8/1/88.

7. Implement changes, monitor for effectiveness, and report results. Smith, 10/15/88.

PROCESS ENGINEERING
Improve Engineering Change Controls

Purpose: To improve and ensure product integrity, it is extremely important to control internal and external (customer) changes. Control includes reviewing for completeness, determining affectivities, approving and implementing change. The procedure is to be developed and implemented for use in all engineering and operations areas.

1. Develop and issue new engineering change control and hold procedure. The procedure will encompass internal and external (customer) change and hold requirements that affect parts, tools, raw materials, jobs, processes, and design.

   A. Develop flows to document the actual engineering change controls presently being used by each of the engineering groups. Smith, 5/10/88.

   B. Develop a new engineering change control procedure and flow. Smith, 7/26/88 (60% complete).

      • Included in these procedures will be final guidelines for handling item holds (that is, holds for parts, tools, raw materials, and so on)

C. Adapt procedure to software—use of engineering change numbers, revision levels, effectiveness for product structures (i.e., part, tools, raw material, and so on) routing and jobs (see the following note). Smith, 8/23/88.

Note: At this time requirements to enter in software have not been completely identified and defined. The plan described does not include any programming interfaces.

D. Test system, software user test. Smith, 9/3/88.

E. Develop training material. Smith, 9/16/88.

F. Train as required, software user test (metallurgical quality assurance, others). Smith, 10/11/88.

G. Implement new engineering change control procedure. Smith, 10/11/88.

QUALITY & TECHNOLOGY DEPARTMENT
Implement Cost Reduction and Productivity Improvements Through Identification/Qualification of Components that can be Heat Treated in Building #5 vs. Currently Overloaded Building #3 Facility

Purpose: The heat treatment of certain large, high-volume castings in Building #3 (that is, axles) requires both extended furnace time and oil quench duration, resulting in scheduling difficulties, higher cost, and increased overall throughput time for other castings requiring use of the Building #3 facility.

The purpose of this program is to increase overall heat treat capacity and flexibility by the formal qualification of Building #5 as a suitable alternate heat treat facility.

1. Review with both heat treat department and product engineers to identify large, high-volume part numbers that would be acceptable candidates for evaluation in Building #3 facility. Smith, 10/22/87.

2. Review available Building #5 heat treat fixturing/handling capabilities and select trial part number(s). Intent would be to select trial components most beneficial to increasing versatility. Smith, 10/30/87.

3. Develop cost proposal for desired quench fixture. Note: Trials will still be attempted in existing fixtures to generate preliminary data. Smith, 11/6/87.

4. Implement trial part number(s) and conduct controlled heat treat study in Building #5, gathering required cycle actuals to facilitate subsequent technical and economic analysis. Smith, 12/7/87.

5. Concurrently conduct both the metallurgical and economic evaluation of the trial part number(s). Smith, 1/18/88.

6. Review results, publish findings, and make recommendations to both heat treat and production departments. Smith, 4/9/88.

7. Assess program direction and the potential necessity to expand to other part numbers. Smith, 6/27/88.

DIE ROOM
Expand Tool Review Program

Purpose: The current tool review program includes only hammer dies and special steel dies from front I-beam presses. The following tasks must be completed to allow comprehensive scheduling of all tool kit requirements through the software system. Comprehensive scheduling will allow the time necessary to provide "no compromise" tools to the forge shop.

The die review committee consists of representatives from the following areas.

Die room—managers and operating personnel
Die design—supervisor or senior die designer
Forge shop—managers and operating personnel
Forge shop engineering—engineer and/or technician
Product assurance—supervisor or senior inspector

Each area representative provides information relative to the performance of the tools being reviewed from the last shop release. Appropriate action is developed, necessary orders generated, and tool status updated in inventory.

1. Develop and implement procedure for post-run review of tooling.
   Knuckle tools—Smith, 2/15/87.
   Extrusion tools—Smith, 10/1/87.
   Trim tools—Smith, 7/1/87.
   Heat treat fixtures—Smith, 2/1/88.

2. Perform physical inventory of all tools and components, and track the percentage of completion. 11/1/88.
   Trim tools—Smith, 70% complete.
   Extrude tools main die room—Smith, 40% complete.
   Tool components Building #5—Smith, 80% complete.

3. Develop process flow diagrams for all tool and die review procedures. Analyze current tool and die review procedures and correct as required.
   Die review—Smith, 6/7/88.
   Heat treat fixture and extrude tool review—Smith, 8/1/88.
   Trim tool review—Smith, 8/1/88.
   Front I-beam die review, Smith, 9/1/88.

4. Department head will audit various die and tool committee meetings. Smith, start 5/1/88.

DIE ROOM
Upgrade and Improve Die Manufacturing Equipment

Purpose: The age and condition of vital die manufacturing equipment limits the ability to produce dies and tools with stricter tolerance requirements. Necessary levels of dimensional quality are not obtainable without costly secondary operations. The quality assurance measuring equipment in the die room is not reliable and requires upgrading.

In addition to the improvement in overall quality of dies and tools, a reduction in subcontracting costs will be realized in 1987. Subcontracting costs for dies and tools will be reduced $_____ in 1988 and subsequent years.

1. Replace (1) small engine lathe, (1) large engine lathe, and (1) turret lathe with (1) small CNC lathe and (1) large CNC lathe. Develop economic justification. Smith, 4/15/88.
   Appropriation request—4/15/88.
   Projected installation:
   Small CNC lathe—12/1/88.
   Large CNC lathe—3/1/89.

2. Rigid mill—rebuild (1) Johnson milling machine. Identify sources for rebuilding the machine tool. Smith, 10/1/87. On schedule.
   Develop request for funds. Smith, 11/1/87. On schedule.
   Initiate rebuild. Smith, 2nd quarter 1988.

3. Purchase (1) large-capacity copy mill.
   Develop bids for large copy mill. Smith, on hold.
   Initiate appropriation request.

4. Replace (1) mid-size vertical turret lathe.
   Identify remanufacturing sources and new equipment sources. Smith, 12/1/87.
   Initiate replacement. Smith, 2nd quarter 1988.

5. 1021 Rebuild. Two bids received to date are unrealistic. Pursuing additional bids. Smith, 3/31/88.

    Initiate appropriation request. Smith, 7/1/88.

    Place order. Hold.

6. 725 Vertical die sinker rebuild.

    Identify sources for rebuilding the machine tool. Smith, 6/1/88.

    Initiate appropriation request. Smith, 11/1/88.

HEAT TREAT DEPARTMENT
Heat Treat Tooling Control

Purpose: Establish a control system to ensure that there are adequate quantities of department-furnished tooling; that is, furnace trays, spider trays, and fixtures are on hand to prevent delays in starting or completing a job.

1. Take an inventory of trays, spiders, and fixtures. Smith, 4/23/87.

2. Determine the number of furnace trays that should be on hand and in good operating condition. Smith, 4/23/87. Bring on-hand quantity up to date. 6/20/87.

3. Determine the number of 20-inch, 26-inch, and 40-inch "faced" spider trays that should be kept on hand. Smith, 4/16/87. Bring on-hand quantity up to date. 6/27/87.

4. Stock authorize each size of spider tray and determine the number to keep on hand in stores and receiving. Smith. Stock authorization form completed and going through the system. "Cards" sent from stores to purchasing, 7/9/87.

5. Develop departmental procedure to inventory trays on a three-month basis. Smith, 1/17/88.

BUILDING #5
Improve Condition and Reliability of Equipment

Purpose: Improve condition, repeatability, and accuracy of all Building #5 machining equipment. The current poor condition of certain machines in Building #5 prevents operators from achieving the required quality of machined parts. Machine condition will be addressed by the following actions.

1. Develop ongoing machine review and repair program to improve the operating conditions of machines, rebuild worn-out equipment, convert machines to CNC controls, or replace obsolete equipment.

   A. Survey all machine operators in Building #5 for 1988 to get their opinions as to the condition of their machines. Smith, 1/25/88.

   B. Repair items identified by the operator survey that can be repaired within the operating requirements of Building #5 machining. Smith, complete by 8/5/88.

   C. Review rebuild/repair requirements for all Building #5 equipment for cost and time constraints. Include consideration to convert to CNC where applicable or replace with new equipment. Smith. Replacing obsolete machine equipment will be part of the 1988 capital expenditure budget.

   D. Prioritize machine repair requirements and develop target dates for the continuation of rebuilding and upgrading of all Building #5 equipment. Smith.

   E. Set up preventive maintenance schedule for machines in PM Building #5. Smith, 4/15/88. Part of department procedure.

2. Repeat steps A through D every six months to ensure that upgrading of equipment is an ongoing process. Smith.

BUILDING #5
Update Equipment to New CNC Controls

Purpose: Upgrade large turning equipment and create additional capacity for CNC turning. Programs continue to increase demands for close tolerance turning equipment.

1. #175 14-ft. vertical boring mill. Update obsolete CNC controls.

   A. Complete/approve appropriation request. Smith, 7/9/87.

   B. Order controls. Smith, ordered 7/9/87.

   C. Shut down for removal. Smith, 9/7/87.

   D. Dismantle/remove machine (use an outside contractor). Smith, 9/19/87.

   E. Rebuild and install new CNC controls. Smith, 1/28/88.

   F. Reinstall machine. Smith. Started 1/21/88; expect completion 3/15/88.

   G. Dry run machine. Smith, 3/28/88.

   H. Machine is fully operational. Smith, 4/22/88.

   I. Train operators. 3 by 6/1/88 and 3 by 9/1/88.

2. #176 and #177 14-ft. vertical boring mills. Update obsolete CNC controls.

   A. Request appropriation. Smith, 9/17/87.

   B. Appropriation request approval. Smith, 11/15/87.

   C. Balance of work to follow rebuild of #175.

PRODUCTION MACHINE
Consolidate Jaws and Kickers into Crib

Purpose: Incorporate jaws and kickers into PM crib to improve and expedite the preparation of tool kits. This action will also provide control of these items and ensure that software information is updated to allow continuity so all operations can be set up properly the first time.

1. Review and compile listing on all established floor bins relating to jaws and kickers and submit weekly to tool engineering. Smith. Start 3/15/88; complete 6/15/88.

2. Evaluate three areas individually for retention, scrap, or re-identification of jaws and kickers, and update software information. Smith.
   CNC machines—Start 5/1/88; complete 8/1/88.
   VTL machines—Start 8/1/88; complete 11/1/88.
   Turning machines—Start 11/1/88; complete 2/1/89.

3. Physically scrap identified jaws and kickers, and evaluate the expansion required in crib to house these items. Smith.
   CNC machines—Start 6/1/88; complete 9/1/88.
   VTL machines—Start 9/1/88; complete 12/1/88.
   Turning machines—Start 12/1/88; complete 3/1/89.

4. Make layout for the expanded facilities needed for crib. Smith. Start 11/1/88; complete 1/15/89.

5. Provide labor and supplies to physically expand crib per layout provided by facility engineering. Smith. Complete 2/1/89.

6. Provide and exercise usage of automated data input (bar coding). Smith. Start 8/1/88; complete 1/15/89.

7. Assemble tool kits upon receipt of software Picklist (24 to 48 hours in advance of setup) and provide as requested by production machine. Smith.

CNC machines—Start 9/1/88; ongoing.

VTL machines—Start 12/1/88; ongoing.

Turning machines—Start 3/1/89; ongoing.

STEEL STORES DEPARTMENT
Upgrade Radius Grind Units

Purpose: Radius grinding on all high-temperature mults is a labor-intensive operation requiring various sizes of radii. Program will utilize input from operators and develop a unit to improve productivity, the accuracy of radius size, and the quality of mults delivered to forging operations.

1. Review the present process to determine the accuracy of radius and output per hour on mult sizes up to 9-inch diameter. Smith/employees, 3/14/87.

2. Develop ideas with hourly personnel, outlining requirements for a new radius grinding unit. Smith, 5/1/87.

3. Interview engineering department and outside sources for design of unit. Smith, 5/18/87.

4. Review all drawings, estimates, and deliveries with purchasing and engineering for approval of unit. Smith/employees, 5/25/87.

5. Purchase and install unit. Smith. Problems with chuck. Purchasing and vendor to submit changes by 10/8/87. Unit malfunctioned first week of operation. Chuck redesigned. Table at vendor, 11/30/87; complete, 2/11/88.

6. Report and monitor quality and rejects/output per hour improvements, document rejected radius, and monitor increased output against manual radius operations. Smith/employees, ongoing. Increased productivity and cost savings projection for 1988 to be completed by 7/31/88. Smith.

Additional Readings

The list that follows has been selected to provide a variety of viewpoints on continuous improvement in manufacturing. It is not meant to be exhaustive.

ASQC Quality Press and Xerox Corporation. *A World of Quality.* Milwaukee, Wis.: ASQC Quality Press; Rochester, N.Y.: Xerox Corporation, 1993.

Bakerjian, Ramon, ed. *Tool and Manufacturing Engineers' Handbook, Volume 7: Continuous Improvement.* Dearborn, Mich.: Society of Manufacturing Engineers, 1993.

Camp, Robert C. *Benchmarking.* Milwaukee, Wis.: ASQC Quality Press; White Plains, N.Y.: Quality Resources, 1989.

Cartin, Thomas J. *Principles and Practices of TQM.* Milwaukee, Wis.: ASQC Quality Press, 1993.

Ciampa, Dan. *Total Quality: A User's Guide for Implementation.* New York: Addison-Wesley, 1992.

Crosby, Philip B. *Quality Is Free.* New York: McGraw-Hill, 1979.

Dauch, Richard E. *Passion for Manufacturing.* Dearborn, Mich.: Society of Manufacturing Engineers, 1993.

Deming, W. Edwards. *Out of the Crisis*. Cambridge, Mass.: Massachusetts Institute of Technology, Center for Advanced Engineering Study, 1986.

Eureka, William E., and Nancy E. Ryan. *The Customer Driven Company*. Dearborn, Mich.: ASI Press, 1988.

Galloway, Dianne. *Mapping Work Processes*. Milwaukee, Wis.: ASQC Quality Press, 1994.

Goldratt, Eliyahu M., and Jeff Cox. *The Goal*. Croton-on-Hudson, N.Y.: North River Press, 1984.

Hammer, Michael, and James Champy. *Reenginneering The Corporation*. New York: HarperCollins, 1993.

Harmon, Roy L. *Reinventing the Factory II*. New York: Free Press, 1992.

Harmon, Roy L., and Leroy D. Peterson. *Reinventing the Factory*. New York: Free Press, 1990.

Hartzler, Meg, and Jane E. Henry. *Team Fitness*. Milwaukee, Wis.: ASQC Quality Press, 1994.

Hay, E. *The Just-In-Time Breakthrough*. New York: Wiley & Sons, 1988.

Hoffman, Peter J. *The ESD Process Improvement Guide*. Hanscom Air Force Base, Mass.: Electronic Systems Division, Air Force Systems Command, 1991.

Hutton, David W. *The Change Agents' Handbook*. Milwaukee, Wis.: ASQC Quality Press, 1994.

Juran, J. M., ed. *Juran's Quality Control Handbook*. New York: McGraw-Hill, 1988.

Juran, J. M. *Juran on Leadership for Quality*. New York: Free Press, 1989.

Kotter, J. *The Leadership Factor*. New York: Free Press, 1988.

Lawler, Edward E. *Pay and Organization Development.* Reading, Mass.: Addison-Wesley, 1981.

Lowenthal, Jeffrey N. *Reengineering the Organization.* Milwaukee, Wis.: ASQC Quality Press, 1994.

Miller, George L., and Larue L. Krumm. *The Whats, Whys and Hows of Quality Improvement.* Milwaukee, Wis.: ASQC Quality Press, 1992.

Monden, Yashuhiro. *Toyota Production System.* Norcross, Ga.: Institute of Industrial Engineers, 1983.

P. A. Consulting Group. *The Total Quality Experience.* Hightstown, N.J.: P. A. Consulting Group, 1991.

Robert, Michel. *Strategy, Pure and Simple.* New York: McGraw-Hill, 1993.

Sandras, William A. *Just In Time: Making It Happen.* Essex Junction, Vt.: Oliver Wight, 1989.

Scholtes, Peter R. *The Team Handbook.* Madison, Wis.: Joiner Associates, 1988.

Umble, M. Michael, and M. L. Srikanth. *Synchronous Manufacturing.* Cincinnati: South-Western Publishing, 1990.

Wantuck, Kenneth A. *Just In Time for America.* Milwaukee, Wis.: The Forum, 1989.

Wellins, Richard S., William C. Byham, and Jeanne M. Wilson. *Empowered Teams: Creating Self-Directed Work Groups that Improve Quality, Productivity, and Participation.* San Francisco: Jossey-Bass Publishers, 1991.

Wilson, Paul F., Larry D. Dell, and Gaylord F. Anderson. *Root-Cause Analysis.* Milwaukee, Wis.: ASQC Quality Press, 1993.

Zuckerman, Marilyn R., and Lewis J. Hatala. *Incredibly American.* Milwaukee, Wis.: ASQC Quality Press, 1992.

Index